Early maths

Longman early childhood education

Marion Dowling *The modern nursery*

David Evans *Sharing sounds*

Hilda Meers *Helping our children talk*

Early maths

Cynthia G. Dawes

Longman London and New York

Longman Group Limited
London and New York
Associated companies, branches and representatives throughout the world

First published 1977

ISBN 0 582 25013 7 cased edition
ISBN 0 582 25012 9 paper edition

Library of Congress Cataloging in Publication Data

Dawes, Cynthia G.
Early maths.

(Longman early childhood education series)
Bibliography: p.91.
Includes index.
1. Mathematics – Study and teaching (Preschool)
I. Title.
QA135.5.D33 372.7 75-42258
ISBN 0-582-25013-7
ISBN 0-582-25012-9 pbk.

Printed in Great Britain by
T. & A. Constable Ltd, Edinburgh

Contents

To the teachers who come to Madeley College on the one-term course in Nursery Work, especially those who came in 1975

Introduction

The Plowden Report (1966) recommended that expanded nursery education should be available for children from three to five and was followed by the James Report and the Government's White Paper (1972). This emphasized the importance of the education of children under five and announced as a target that places were to be provided in schools for 90% of the four-year-olds and 50% of the three-year-olds, with 15% of these age groups attending full-time and the rest part-time. This, it was stated, should be achieved by 1981. Since the publication of this White Paper, the Secretary of State for Education has repeatedly stressed the Government's support for the expansion of nursery provision despite financial restrictions. Many L.E.A.s are acting on this and planning new nursery schools or nursery units to be attached to existing infant or first schools. The D.E.S. Report on Education No.82 attempted to give projected figures for the number of under-fives in school within the next decade. These will depend not only on the probable number of births within the next few years but also on the extent to which parents are inclined to send their children to nursery schools. Even allowing for caution in attempting such predictions, the increase in the number of children attending nursery schools is thought to be in the range of 200,000 by the 1980s.

Many more trained nursery teachers will be needed to staff the new nursery schools and many more N.N.E.B. trained nursery assistants will be needed to help them. Those teachers and assistants must be trained specifically for this age range. This will mean the allocation of more places for would-be nursery school teachers in our colleges of education, polytechnics etc., an expansion of N.N.E.B. training and the re-training of many serving teachers or married women returning to teaching who had originally trained to teach older children. Head teachers of those infant and first schools to which the new nursery units will be attached will also need to be made aware of their aims and objectives and to understand the work suitable for children of three to five years. Training establishments are therefore planning and implementing new nursery courses both for initial training and in the in-service field. A natural corollary to this increase in nursery training is the need for books covering the whole range of the development of the pre-school child. One area that appears not to be well documented is that of mathematics in the nursery school. Yet the first four years of a child's life is one of the most important periods in the development of his intellect. It has been proved that we can influence a person's intelligence most at periods of growth and during the pre-school years a child's brain reaches its highest physiological efficiency. How vitally important these years could be to mathematical development!

Unfortunately in many nursery schools mathematics is either ignored or those children who appear to be able to count and to recognize a few numbers are pushed on to do the type of mathematics more suitable for the infant school. This is mainly due to a lack of understanding by the teacher of both the development of mathematical thinking and of the mental ability of the nursery child. The intention of this book is first to examine how a child's ability to think mathematically develops, then to discuss what mathematical experiences are relevant to his stage of development and then to examine where and when these experiences can take place in the nursery school. Since it is not sufficient for any teacher just to know what can be done at a particular stage but she must also understand why it is being done and what could develop from it, we shall go on to look at these experiences to see why they are important to the future development of the child's mathematical understanding.

To most people, mathematics seems to mean the ability to understand numbers and to be able to perform operations with numbers. Certainly number is a most important part of mathematics and because of this the child's approach to number is dealt with first. But experiences in other sections of mathematics are also discussed and the suitability of experiences involving shape and spatial concepts for the nursery child is stressed. It is hoped that this book will be of use to all training for work with the pre-school child whether they are in initial training or following in-service courses. It is also hoped that headteachers will find it helpful as they widen their responsibilities to include the children and the teachers in their nursery units and that parents will find that it will help them to understand the value of some of the experiences of their children at nursery school or that it helps them to supply helpful experiences for those children who remain at home during their pre-school years.

Cynthia G. Dawes
May 1975

Since writing this introduction there have been far-reaching changes in the whole educational field. Due to financial stringencies the expansion of nursery education has suffered a substantial setback.

Despite this, with the continuing increase in the number of working mothers, there is an urgent need for well-informed playgroup leaders and childminders as well as the fully trained nursery teachers in areas where finances are being made available for nursery expansion. I hope that this book will prove to be readable and helpful to all those engaged in looking after the pre-school child.

1

The development of mathematical thinking*

It is not sufficient merely to discuss the mathematics that is suitable for the nursery school child. We must first look at what we mean by mathematics and then at how mathematical thinking develops.

What is mathematics?

Mathematics is concerned with structures and relationships. The operation of multiplication affords a simple example of what is meant by mathematical structure. Multiplication is a binary operation, that is only two numbers can be multiplied at a time. When a child is confronted with the need to multiply more than two numbers he therefore must associate these numbers in pairs. The way in which he associates them does not matter e.g. $2\times4\times5$ can be achieved by associating 2 and 4 together and then multiplying by 5, or by associating 2 and 5 and then multiplying by 4 or by associating 4 and 5 together and then multiplying by 2.

i.e. $2\times4\times5=(2\times4)\times5=(2\times5)\times4=(4\times5)\times2$

The child can choose which of these he prefers. This is a piece of structure referred to as 'the associative property of multiplication'.

A relationship means any connection that exists between the members of one set and those of another. A graph made by children that shows their favourite pets is a pictorial representation of the relationship 'prefers' between the set of children in the class and the set of pets (see Fig 1.1). Similarly the set of numbers (1, 2, 3, 4 – – – –) is connected to the set (1, 4, 9, 16 – – – –) by the relationship 'is the positive square root of'.

One of the best definitions of mathematics is that it is the recognition and the study of patterns. These patterns refer to any regularity that our minds can recognize. They could be patterns of numbers e.g. the pattern of the table of nines. It will often help children who find it difficult to learn by rote to remember this table if they recognize the pattern within it. If we examine the table: 9, 18, 27, 36, 45, 54, 63, 72, 81, 90, 99, 108, (why do we usually stop at

*A glossary of mathematical terms is provided on pp 86 90.

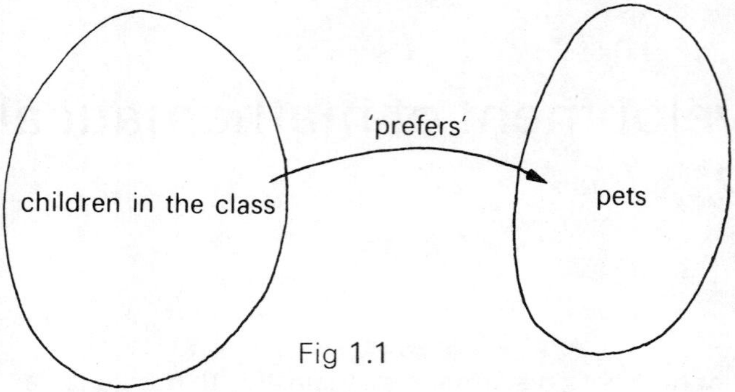

Fig 1.1

twelve sets?) we notice that the units digit goes down one each time whilst the tens digit goes up one. Also, the tens digit (until ninety-nine) is always one less than the number of nines i.e. in six nines the tens digit is five. If we add the digits we find that their sum is always nine (except for ninety-nine when the sum is eighteen, but the second digit sum is nine!) If a child needs to know, say, seven nines, these facts will help him. The tens digit will be one less than seven i.e. six, and the sum of the digits will be nine so the units digit will be 9–6 i.e. 3. So the answer to his problem is $7 \times 9 = 63$.

Mathematics can also be the study of patterns in shape e.g. the symmetry of an iris head, which is seen to be the same as that of an equilateral triangle (see Fig 1.2); or the tessellation of isosceles

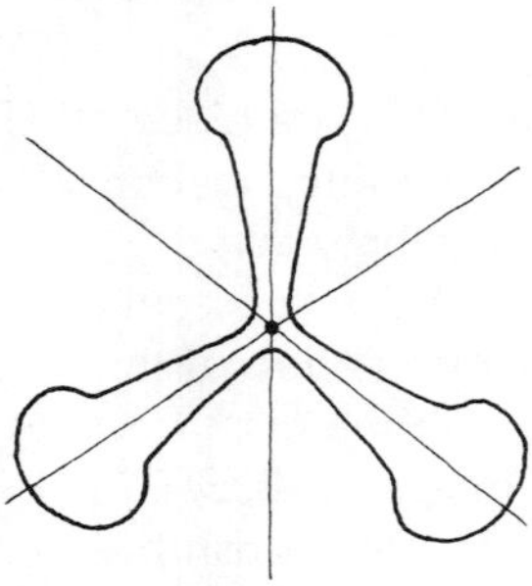
Fig 1.2

right-angled triangles which can lead a child to an initial discovery of a special case of Pythagoras' Theorem and hence to an investigation of whether this theorem holds for any triangle (see Fig 1.3). This investigation can be by means of yet another shape pattern, the tessellation of two different sized squares which leads to Perigal's dissection (see Fig 1.4). Mathematics could be patterns of movement such as the pattern traced out by a ball thrown up in the air or a missile fired from a catapult (see Fig 1.5).

Fig 1.3

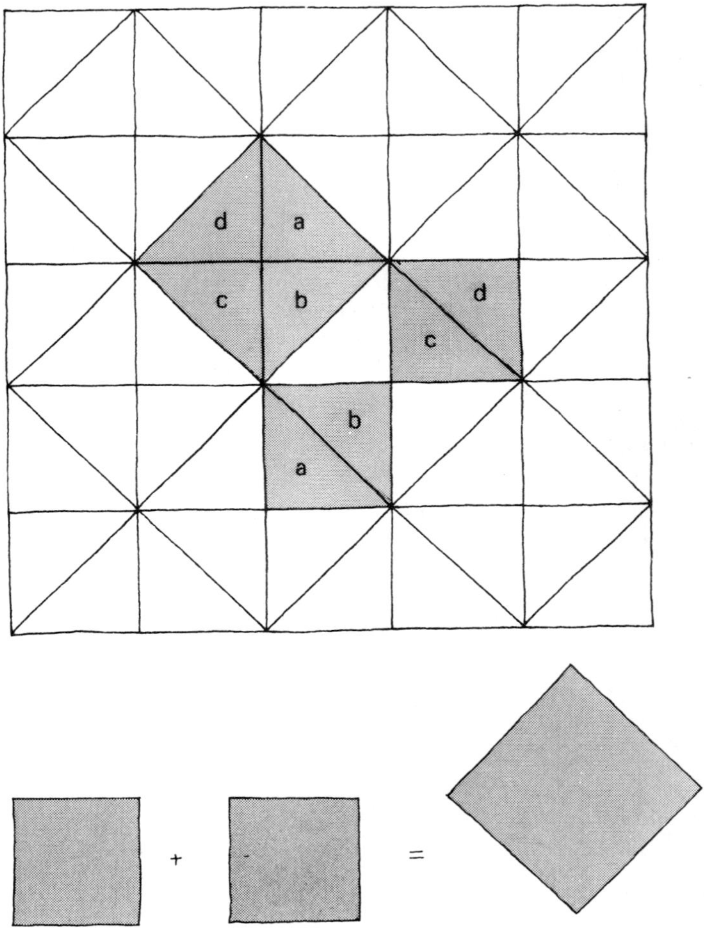

'Modern Maths'

In the past most people equated mathematics with the ability to juggle with numbers quickly and to produce the correct answer. This number work is still a vital part of mathematics but nowadays we tend to widen the mathematical experiences of young children to include other sections of the subject suitable for their mental development. The whole emphasis in mathematics has also changed. Often in the past children produced correct answers by applying rules that had been learned but not understood. The emphasis was on the teacher teaching while the children sat quietly in rows supposedly taking it all

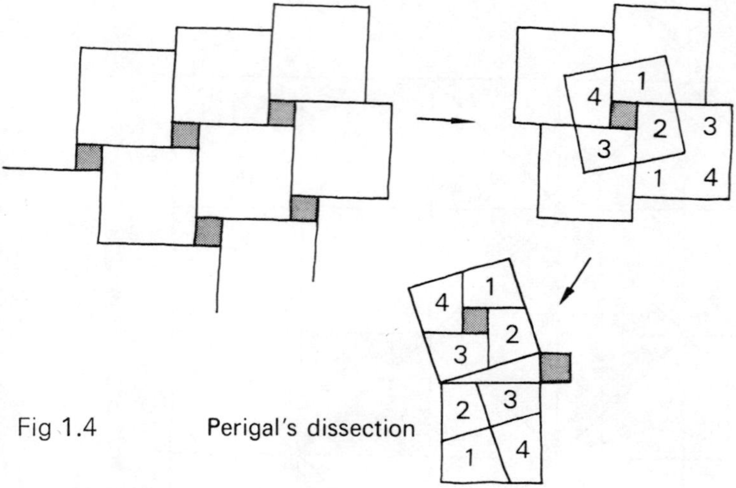

Fig 1.4 Perigal's dissection

in. During the last thirty years there has been a revolution in the teaching of mathematics and there has emerged what many claim to be a new subject called 'Modern Mathematics'. Many teachers of older pupils blame this new subject for their pupils' apparent lack of skill in performing formal calculations and the press often carries

Fig 1.5

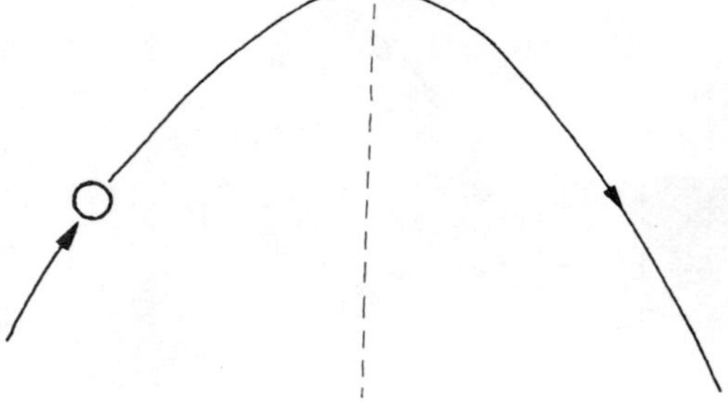

articles on the damage being done by this 'New Maths'. Like so many gimmicks in education today, 'Modern Maths' has been hailed by some teachers as a band-wagon to jump aboard without realizing that the shift in emphasis in the subject requires a complete re-thinking of their teaching techniques and that unless the new methods are understood and used responsibly the results will be just as bad as those already produced by poor teachers and nothing like as effective as those produced by the good teacher using traditional methods. So there is no new subject but a shift in emphasis from the teacher teaching to the child learning. How, then, does the child learn?

In very simple terms there are five main stages in the way in which a child learns:

Developmental stages

Stage 1 covers the span from birth to approximately eighteen months. During this stage the child learns through what happens to him. He has no words to think with but he learns to anticipate experiences from the actions that precede them e.g. he stops crying as his mother lifts him up because this action often precedes the pleasing experience of feeding.

Stage 2 is roughly from eighteen months to four years. (These age spans are indistinct as all children are so very different and, just as they all cut their teeth at different times, so they will pass from one stage to another as individuals.) Now the child is beginning to use symbols, i.e. representations, in the form of language (he is learning to talk), imaginative play (he is acting out happenings) and drawing.

Stage 3 from four years to approximately seven years is the time when the child begins to make judgements about size, shape and relationships. These judgements are based on his own experiences and are often made without reasoning and so are often incorrect.

Stage 4, seven to twelve years, is when the child starts to think logically so long as he is helped by contact with concrete materials and real situations.

Stage 5 from twelve onwards is a stage not achieved by all children i.e. some adults remain in Stage 4. Now the child is able to carry out logical operations in the abstract. He is able to reason his way through a complicated problem and come to a logical conclusion.

Stages 1 to 3 are those which are most important to the nursery teacher. We must explore how experiences within these stages can help the child's mathematical thinking develop. Psychologists have made extensive studies of the development of thought in children during this century. Perhaps the psychologist who has contributed more than any other to our understanding of the development of mathematical thinking is Piaget. From his work we realize that children do not think in the same way as adults do and we must neither expect them to do so nor must we try to make them. Many young teachers find this very difficult to understand and it is here that the detailed study of one particular child over a long period, listening to what he has to say to his friends, his teacher and himself, watching his reactions to different situations and observing his drawings and play-acting can help the young teacher or student to really get 'inside' the child's head and 'listen' to his thinking. The complex processes of thought are acquired gradually, developing from extremely simple forms found in the very young infant.

Constancy of objects

Through handling objects and talking about them the child can be led to discover that things still exist even when he cannot see them. Here he is establishing a mental picture which is one prerequisite of thinking. He will also become aware of the constancy of objects despite their apparent change in size or shape through distance and change of viewpoint. So often we take it for granted that the young child can cope with this sort of thing. (A young friend provided a good example of this when we took him to Whipsnade Zoo. As we approached the zoo we pointed out the lion cut into the hillside. Stevie, aged four, looked in vain for a lion. His conception of a lion was a tawny brown animal prowling on the hill and what he saw was a patch of bald hillside! His view of the Whipsnade Lion was not ours. Gradually he recognized the characteristics as we pointed them out and gleefully he agreed there *was* a lion on the hill. We drove on and a little later as we turned a bend in the road Stevie shouted 'There's another lion'. This time it was we who looked in vain – it was the same lion seen from a different viewpoint. When we said it was the same one, Stevie thought a moment and then said 'Well, it must have moved' in a tone of voice that said 'That settles that!')

Through the young child's play with objects and through drawing his attention to objects as he moves around them we must check that he is aware of their constancy before we can develop further experiences that need this understanding.

Through carrying out activities with actual objects such as building with toy bricks, setting the table in the wendy house for a dolls' tea party, dressing dolls or making pictures from felt shapes, the young child is foreshadowing with concrete materials the imaginative operations which are the beginnings of logical thought. By following through chains of such actions and then reversing this chain he is anticipating the experiments that he will later carry out in his mind in the abstract. This is what Piaget refers to as the logic of action which precedes the logic of thought.

Piaget's experiment

One particular experiment that Piaget tried with young children helps us to understand the pre-school child's mental state. It must be emphasized that this is only one such experiment among hundreds that Piaget has used but it seems particularly relevant to the study of the development of mathematical thought. This is the experiment where Piaget put out in front of the child seven eggcups in a row and asked him to take enough eggs to fill the cups and put them down in front of the cups. Many people ask why Piaget used eggs and eggcups. He was, as all good teachers would, using something with which the children were familiar and objects which naturally go together in the child's mind. He discovered that there were three quite distinct stages in the child's reactions.

At the nursery school age, the majority of children took some eggs and made a row in front of the cups as long as the row of cups

Fig 1.6

(see Fig 1.6). The child did not do what you and I would do and either count the cups and so take the same number of eggs or match the eggs to the cups. Piaget then took the eggs one at a time and put them in the cups and the child was surprised to see that there were too many. But he agreed with Piaget that there were certainly too many and allowed Piaget to remove the extra ones. Then, in front of the child, Piaget took the eggs out of the cups and, instead of putting them out in a row, he piled them up in a heap. He then asked the child if there were enough eggs for the egg cups and at this stage of development the child said 'No', although he had seen them in the cups and watched Piaget remove them.

What does this tell us about the child's stage of mathematical thinking? It tells us that at pre-school age the majority of children cannot make what we call a one–one correspondence i.e. they cannot match one egg to each cup, and they also cannot recognize the constancy of number. Although they can agree that there are the right number of eggs when they see them in the cups, they cannot recognize that the number remains the same when the eggs are removed and re-arranged. A child who is at this stage is not really capable of counting, although he may be able to recite his numbers, since counting depends on being able to make a one–one correspondence between a number name and an object. We all know the little girl who comes to nursery school and proudly claims 'I can count' but when asked to count the fingers on her hand, solemnly chants 'One, two, three, four, five, six, seven' and does not match one with the first finger, two with the second etc. The child is most certainly not at the stage when he can be expected to operate with numbers, i.e. add or subtract, if he cannot even recognize their constancy.

At the second stage, that of the reception class in infant school, the majority of children took one egg and put it in front of each cup i.e. they could make a one–one correspondence, but when Piaget altered the configuration of the eggs either by piling them together or by spreading them out in a longer row, these children still thought there were too few or too many eggs. So, at this stage, most children are still incapable of recognizing the constancy of number. Some children are still in this stage at six or seven and so we are wrong to expect these, even at this age, to be able to cope with much in the way of operations with numbers although in most classes these children will be expected to cope with tens and units! It is no wonder that children like this who are forced on too soon never really learn to cope with mathematics!

The final stage Piaget found usually follows pretty quickly on the second. This is when the child can make a one–one correspondence and when the arrangement of the eggs is altered looks at his questioner in surprise, and often scathing superiority, and says 'Of course there are enough eggs, I put them in the cups.' Here the child is not only recognizing the constancy of number but is showing his ability to reverse the thinking process. It is only when he reaches this stage that he is ready to progress to the beginnings of addition etc. Many teachers and students feel this experiment is rather ludicrous until they have tried it themselves with young children. There are certainly many opportunities in the nursery school for the teacher to observe children in similar situations so that the child's ability to attempt a one–one correspondence or to recognize the constancy of number can be noted.

From this experiment and many similar ones Piaget came to some conclusions that are very meaningful for mathematics. He decided that children learn mathematical concepts far more slowly than we had realized and that they learn through their own activities; they all think and reason in different ways but they all pass through certain stages which depend not only on both their chronological and their mental ages but also on their experiences; we can accelerate their learning by providing them with suitable experiences; children need practice but this should follow and not precede discovery. Throughout the child's educational experience we should keep these conclusions well in mind so that we never force a child on to the next stage until he is really ready; we involve him in discovery; we provide him with experiences that will help him to learn. This means that he must be given opportunity for experimenting, for making his own judgements no matter how illogical they appear at the early stages, for expressing things in his own words and for solving problems in his own way.

Number activities

There are three activities in which we must involve the young child which are absolutely vital to his understanding of number. The first of these is the activity of sorting or classifying into sets. This will lead him to a recognition of the cardinal number of a set i.e. to the answer to the question 'how many?'. The second is that of making the one–one correspondence that we have mentioned earlier and which leads the child to the ability to count and the third is that of putting things in order which will help the child in the ordering of numerals. In the next chapter we investigate these in detail and see what opportunities for these activities can be made possible in the nursery school.

2
Pre-number experiences

Sorting and sets

Sorting or classification is the basis of all logical thought. If we want to solve a problem of any kind we must first sort the information available to us. For instance, if we are reading a detective novel and are trying to work out for ourselves who was guilty of the crime we must sort the clues that are given us. Some of these clues will indicate that it was probably the butler that did it, some will indicate that Aunt May was guilty, others will indicate the guilt of other people while some will show that various people probably were not guilty. Only by sorting this information carefully can we come to any logical conclusion. Faced with shopping for the weekend meals we must sort the various possibilities, sort the various costs and cash available; faced with the family wash we sort the articles into loads for the machine requiring similar washing programmes; our adult lives are full of sorting situations. The infant child learning to write will be encouraged to sort letters into those that 'go up and down' and those that 'go round'. When he is learning to read he may sort out words that begin with a particular sound. In junior school a child needing to find the lowest common multiple of 2, 3 and 5 can sort the counting numbers into those which are divisible by 2, those which are divisible by 3 and those which are divisible by 5. The first number that he finds that belongs to all three of these classifications will be the L.C.M. that he needs (see Fig 2.1). The secondary school pupil confronted with a geometrical problem must look for sets of equal angles, sets of parallel lines etc. Sorting, then, occurs throughout a child's school life and throughout his adult life. It is essential for logical thought and so is the foundation of mathematics.

Also it will be through sorting concrete articles, buttons, counters, small toys, shapes etc. into sets that the infant child will be helped to understand what is meant by the cardinal number of a set. Through sorting he is led to the answer to the question 'how many?' Numbers are very much like colours. If we want to show a child what is meant by green we can only do this by showing him examples of green-ness. 'Here is a green apple. John has a green pullover on today. This pencil

Fig 2.1

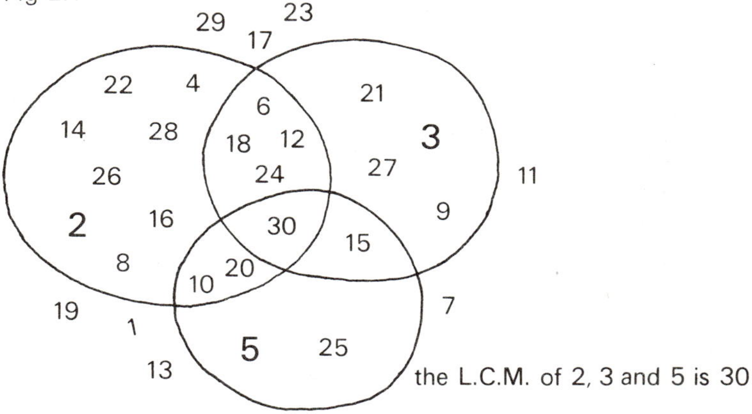

is green. Mary's pencil case is green.' By looking at these examples of green objects the child gradually abstracts the common property of green-ness. Similarly with numbers. If we are helping a child to recognize three, we show him sets of three; three toy cars, three buttons, three children at the sand-tray, three bricks, until he abstracts the common property of three-ness.

Sorting is a very natural activity. People often say that they cannot understand 'Modern Mathematics' because they do not understand all 'this set language'! But the idea of a set is something that we are all very familiar with. We all know what is meant by a tea-set or a train-set or a chemistry-set and the word set is used in exactly the same way in mathematics; it just means a well-defined collection. This collection can be of objects, or of ideas, or of people, or numbers, or concepts etc. By well-defined the mathematician means that what belongs to the set can be easily identified e.g. we can make a set of red buttons and it is quite clear that only things that are generally recognized as buttons and that are also red can go into that set. But we might just as easily identify the set of things in my handbag and these have, probably, no other shared property than the fact that they happen to be in my bag at this particular time; none the less they are a well-defined collection.

The role of the teacher

How then can this sorting which is so vital to logical thought and therefore to mathematics fit into the nursery school? It is because it is such a natural activity that it will occur intuitively in the context of the child's play i.e. it will not be the more formalized sorting of the infant school. The role of the teacher or nursery assistant is one of observer and initiator of discussion; encouraging further sorting, and, at the same time, building up the child's vocabulary by using words that the child will, in time, imitate. At this stage the child should be encouraged to sort according to his own classifications rather than directed by the adult but, when the occasion arises, the adult will encourage the child to vocalize his classification. Often this classification will not be the one we expect. For instance, the adult may watch a child collecting together what to the adult eye appears to be red beads (large wooden ones probably) only to see the child include in his collection a larger blue bead. When asked why the child added that particular bead the reply could be: 'Well, the others are all red but I like this one best.' A perfectly logical reason to the child at that particular stage of his development. It is through conversations like this that the teacher can learn about and assess the child's mental growth.

If the opportunity arises to encourage sorting it should be of the pre-testing type. For instance, if we ask a young child to sort out all the red beads we are testing his recognition of red-ness. At the nursery stage it is better to show the child a red bead and ask him to find you another like it. He may select another red bead or he may select another bead, another red object, another wooden object or another object with a hole in it. Again through talking with the child the adult may learn why that particular object was selected and can then encourage the making of a set of similar objects; but it is the child who has chosen the common property of his set and not the adult.

Things to sort

No special apparatus is really necessary for sorting in the nursery school. It is best to let the child use his natural environment, but the good nursery teacher will make sure that within that environment there is plenty of sortable material. In the infant school a very useful piece of sorting apparatus is the set of plastic Attribute Blocks consisting of five different shaped blocks; triangles, squares, rectangles, circles and hexagons, made in three different colours: red, yellow and blue, in two different sizes; big and small, and two different thicknesses. These provide many ways of sorting for the infant and could be provided for the nursery child to play with. At pre-school age, however, the teacher would encourage sorting for one attribute only and avoid if possible the situation where an intersection of sets arises (see Fig 2.2). This is a later development and unless it arises naturally from a child's play it is best left until the infant stage. As we can draw no hard and fast line between the nursery and the infant child, however, we shall find that some nursery children are further advanced than others and will need enrichment experiences. Often the nursery teacher is tempted to push these children along and to begin formalized teaching because the child appears to be ready

Fig 2.2

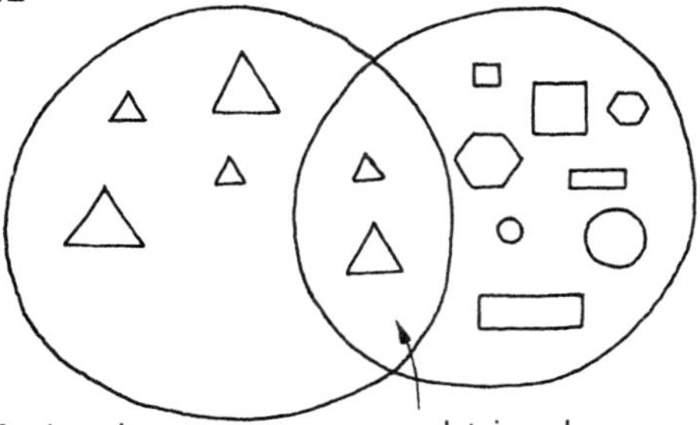

for it. Here we must be very sure that by doing so we are not stretching the child's ability into too fine a thread. It is much better to widen and strengthen the child's experiences than to stretch him too far. What enrichment experiences can we provide for such a child? More sophisticated sorting can be suggested. For example if the child has shown his ability to sort into colours and simple shapes, encourage him to look at the material things are made of. Can he find some wooden things as distinct from plastic or metal? Can he find subsets within the sets that he has made? e.g. if he has collected a set of farmyard animals can he sort these into subsets and name those subsets; which of his subsets consist of animals that fly etc.? Encourage him to find the 'odd man out' in a set where you have planted something without the common attribute of the rest e.g. a set of toy cars with a van included.

Where then shall we find examples of intuitive sorting in the nursery child's natural environment and when shall we find opportunities to encourage further sorting or discuss sorting with him?

Tidying up probably provides the most obvious example of sorting. The young child can be encouraged to tidy up the things he has played with and to return things to their appropriate boxes, containers, cupboards etc. The dressing-up box will provide many opportunities for intuitive sorting. Sorting not only into sets of hats, sets of shoes etc. but also the sorting out of clothes for particular imaginative roles e.g. clothes that make me look like a bride or clothes that make me look like a spaceman. Often as we observe such selections we will see that what was obviously a bridal garment yesterday is just as obviously part of a spaceman's essential equipment today. The wendy house is another rich source of sorting activities. There are the sets of tea things, the sets of cooking pans, sets of chairs, sets of dolls, sets of bedding, sets of cleaning things, but also the set of clothes for a particular doll, the set of bedding for a particular bed e.g. the baby's cot etc. Here also is the opportunity for making a set of plastic things which may include most of the tea set, some of the dolls, some of the brushes and dustpan, the washing up bowl etc.

The children themselves also provide sorting material. They can be sorted into 'my friends', the boys, the girls, those who want to paint, those who are at the sandpit, those who are wearing long trousers today, those with lace-up shoes, those with ribbons in their hair or those with elder brothers or sisters in the infants department. Various occupations will also provide sorting opportunities: painting and drawing will provide sets of brushes, crayons, paints, pencils. Out of these we can encourage the making of sets of different coloured things, sets of things that will make thick lines or thin lines, those that make dark or light markings. The constructional toys will themselves be in sets: sets of bricks, sets of Lego, sets of interlocking cubes, and these again can be cross-sorted into colours, lengths and so on. The music corner will provide instruments that we bang, others that we shake or pluck, but again these can be cross-sorted into metal instruments or round shapes or different colours. At the water trough we will find a set of aprons, sets of containers, sets of things that let the water through e.g. sieves, funnels, colanders, sets of bottles, sets of plastic things, sets of metal things and many others. The actual furniture of the nursery classroom can be sorted and at story time the books on the shelves can be sorted into story books, picture books, books about animals, thick books, little books and books we like.

The stories, rhymes and songs used in the nursery class will also give the children sorting experiences. If we make friezes, collages or any other illustrations of these stories or rhymes we provide more sorting activities; sorting material to find the right piece for the giant's beard, finding shiny things to portray the knight's armour, rough material for the alligator's skin, blue paint for the sky, big thick brushes with which to put the paint on more quickly and so on. All these activities and many more will give the children a valuable beginning to sorting that will lay a good foundation for logical mathematical thought later on.

Simple numbers

We will also be helping the child with the recognition and understanding of simple numbers. Children of this age will be familiar with number names, they will know they live at 'number seven' or they must catch a number 6 bus when they go to town with Mummy, but will have a real understanding of only a few numbers. They will know and understand what is meant by 'one' or by 'two' and will probably know 'three' and maybe 'four'. This familiarity with numbers may be increased through number rhymes and songs or stories. Illustrations of *Three Blind Mice,* the story of *The Three Bears,* the *Three Wise Men* at Christmas and the three ships that 'came sailing in on Christmas Day in the morning' will all help with the recognition of a set of three. The familiarity of young children with numbers, often through space rocket count-downs or games, can make us feel that they understand more than they do. Although the recognition of one, two and three may be quite firm at this stage it will not be secure for numbers like seven or eight until most children are six or even seven. Teachers are often guilty of too readily assuming the recognition of numbers and will force abstractions on to children before they are ready for them. The fact that the child can sing *Ten green bottles* or *One man went to mow* all the way through and recite the blast off count-down certainly does not show that he knows what is meant by eight or nine or that he can count backwards from ten or even that he can count at all!

Zero

If we can build in experiences that will give familiarity with zero at this stage, we will be helping children towards the understanding of what is often a difficult concept. Introduce as naturally as possible the idea of nothing i.e. the idea of an empty set. When tidying up ask the children to give you all the things belonging to a set that you know has no members so that you encourage the remark 'There aren't any'. If you notice that no one in the class is wearing a red jumper on a particular day ask the children if they can tell you how many red jumpers they can see. Act out songs like *Ten green bottles* so that when there are 'No green bottles standing on the wall' their attention is again centred on an empty set. This will help the children to answer for themselves 'What do we mean by nothing?'

Combining sets

Other mathematical processes are based on this introductory work of sorting. Combining sets e.g. putting the set of knives with the set of forks, gives concrete experiences leading to addition later on (logic of action preceding logic of thought). Addition is the mental process arising from the physical operation of taking the objects of one set and putting them together with those of another (see Fig 2.3). This

Fig 2.3

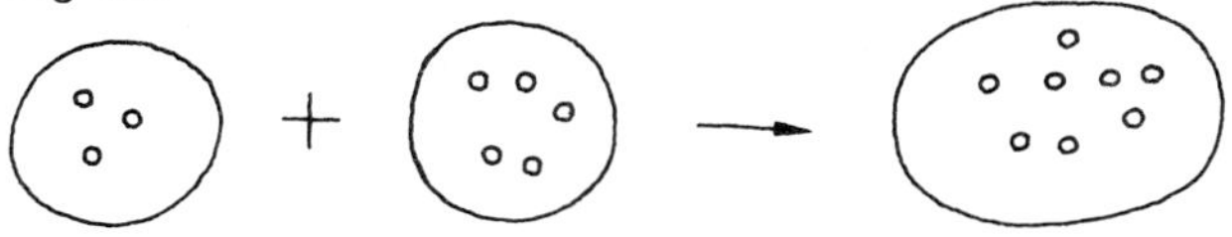

combining of sets also leads on to multiplication which is the operation of putting together equivalent sets i.e. sets of the same cardinal number (see Fig 2.4). The identification of subsets e.g. among the set of water containers is a subset of jugs, will lead on to partitioning later on, i.e. sorting within a set into disjoint subsets (see Fig 2.5). This in

Fig 2.4

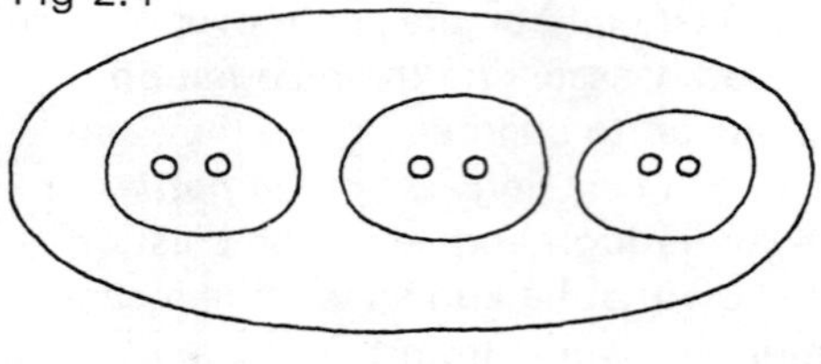

Fig 2.5

Fig 2.6

partitioning according to shape

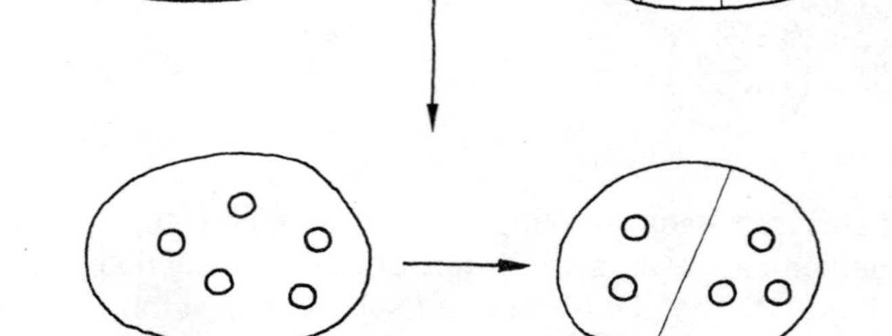

i.e. 2 + 3 → 5

turn could lead the child on to discover part of the story of a number or number bonds (see Fig 2.6).

It is worthwhile attempting to discover whether nursery children can understand the idea of inclusion and giving them experiences which will help them towards this. If a child is involved in some activity where you can recognize a subset of a set e.g. a set of dolls' dresses, some of which are party dresses, discuss this with the child so that you are sure he understands what you mean by party dresses. Then ask him if he has more dresses or more party dresses and at this particular stage he is quite likely to be unable to answer correctly. Until he can answer this type of question confidently and correctly we must not expect him to be able to cope with the mathematical equivalent of this which is division by partitioning, e.g. when finding how many sets of 2 in a set of 6 a child must be able to find particular subsets (sets of 2) within a particular set (a set of 6) (see Fig 2.7).

Fig. 2.7

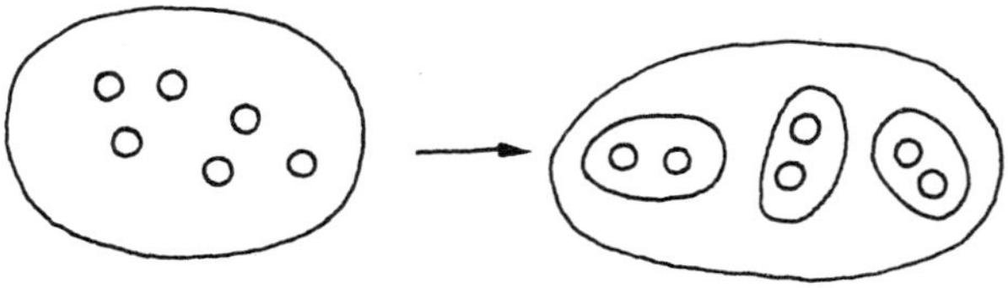

i.e. there are 3 subsets of 2 in a set of 6 or $6 \div 2 \rightarrow 3$

Matching

The second pre-number activity that is vital to mathematics and very suitable for nursery work is that of matching or making a one–one correspondence. This, which we discussed with reference to Piaget's experiment with the eggs and eggcups, is essential for counting. It will also lead the children on to the use of pre-number phrases e.g. 'more than', 'fewer than' and 'the same number as'. Again, these activities should, at this stage, arise naturally from the child's play and will be observed and encouraged by the teacher. As with sorting, they will be dealt with in a more formal manner in the infant school. The nursery teacher must plan the child's environment so that plenty of opportunities are provided for quite natural matching. When the child arrives at nursery school he will hang his coat on his peg i.e. a matching activity, one peg for each child and, probably, one coat on one peg. He will probably match himself to the picture or symbol that is stuck beside that peg. As the child dresses himself he will match a button with each buttonhole on his coat or cardigan.

The wendy house will provide many natural matchings: cups to be matched with saucers, knives matched with forks, plates with spoons, lids for saucepans, a brush in the dustpan etc. Laying a table for a meal, whether it is for the children's own lunch or for a dolls' teaparty, is another chance to practise one–one correspondence. Dolls will be put to bed, one in each bed, and each bed will be matched with a pillow and then with a blanket. The imaginative play that takes place in the wendy house will be full of these opportunities for matching.

Dressing-up is another chance for practice in this activity; one shoe for each foot, one glove for each hand, one hat for each child etc. Children can also be provided with cardboard cut-out dolls to dress or material dolls to place and dress on a flannelgraph. Here, shoes and socks should already be on the cut-out or material doll so that the emphasis can be on one vest for each doll, one pair of pants for each doll, one dress for each doll, one coat, one hat and not two shoes or two socks for each doll. Sets of cards can easily be made by the teacher for matching practice. These can be picture cards that the child matches in pairs from a collection of cards within a box – matched because of the picture or because of colour. For the more able child they could be Bingo type cards which the child covers with matching cards selected from a large collection in a play situation

Fig 2.8

and not in the competitive style of adult Bingo (see Fig 2.8). Matching activity charts can also be made. These need to be large and well constructed so that the children can perform the activity time and time again (see Fig 2.9). Here the child takes the bones out of the

Fig 2.9

pocket and slots one bone into each dog's mouth. Similar charts can be made showing children with teddy bears to be slotted into their arms or clowns with hats to be put on their heads etc. The teacher should, at intervals, change the number of bones, teddies or hats in the pockets so that sometimes there are 'the same number as', sometimes 'not enough', and sometimes 'too many'.

We can also use matching to check situations within the nursery classroom e.g. the number of children at the water trough can be controlled by their matching themselves with a large chart showing the right number of children (probably cut out pictures from magazines). If the teacher has decided that four children are sufficient at the trough in her classroom, she will call attention to the waterplay if she notices more than four children there. The children will then match themselves to the children in the picture and those who cannot be matched will have to choose another occupation and it will be appreciated by the class or the group that there were 'too many' at the trough. Some classes will control the number at the trough by matching children with waterproof aprons; if there are no waterproof aprons left, then there are 'enough' people at the trough. Other classes use matching to record attendance. Each child as he arrives selects a large poppet bead from a box and pops it on to the attendance chain. This chain can then be matched with yesterday's and discussion provoked with the children as to whether there are the same number here today, fewer or more, and then, whether in fact we have the same people here as yesterday since John may have come back to school but Harry may be away today. By using one colour bead for the boys and another for the girls more discussion and comparison could arise.

Drawing and painting activities can also provide experiences of matching. One apron per child, one child to each side of the painting easel, one piece of paper per child, one water pot with one paintbrush and so on. Sitting together at story time could mean one child on one chair or one child on one small mat. Sharing out the results of simple baking will probably be one cake or biscuit for each child and as these cakes are prepared, one cake will be put in one cake-paper or in one bun tin. More experiences of matching will be provided by simple graphical recording mentioned in Chapter 5.

Constancy of number

Matching can be used to help children towards the understanding of the constancy of number referred to in Piaget's experiment with the eggs. If a child seems unsure whether a set of bricks piled together contains more, fewer or the same number of bricks as that same pile re-arranged (perhaps spread out in a long line) then he can be encouraged to match each brick in the pile with a square on a strip of squared paper, by colouring one square for one brick, and then to match each brick in the new configuration with those same squares. This operation involves a chain of actions which could be too complex for some children at this stage but for others it will provide another example of a chain of actions that will precede a chain of thought.

Subtraction

Apart from its connection with counting, pre-number phrases and the constancy of number, matching will be used in many mathematical situations later in the child's education. For instance, matching has importance in subtraction. There are three quite different aspects of subtraction that a child must have experience of, i.e. take away, find the difference and adding on. It is the second of these which needs the ability to make a one–one correspondence. If, for instance, the young child wishes to know how many more marbles he has than his friend, he needs to 'find the difference'. This he and his friend can do by laying their marbles down together and matching across. The unmatched set will then show the difference (see Fig 2.10). Here the child will probably recognize that he has two more (or two less) but if the unmatched set had more than about five marbles in it he would, at this stage, probably be happy to say 'I've got lots more'. Again,

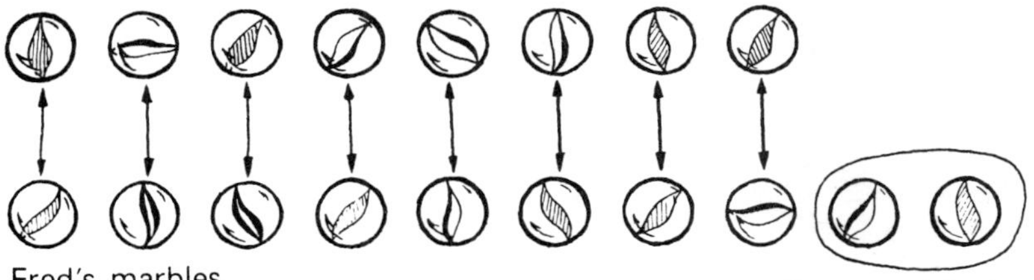

Fig 2.10

reference will be made to the difference between two sets in the chapter on simple recording.

Multiplication
Matching also helps with multiplication later on. Infant children are not introduced to multiplication as a completely new operation; it is based on addition and is the repeated addition of equivalent sets i.e. sets with the same number of members. In order to understand multiplication, then, a child must be able to recognize equivalent sets. He can do this through matching to see that he has 'the same number as'. Practice in recognizing equivalent sets can be given to nursery children by encouraging reference to sets of two e.g. my two eyes, two ears, two arms, two hands, two legs, two feet. When changing for movement the teacher will discuss with a few children their two shoes and two socks and the use of the word 'pair'. A Noah's Ark with all the sets of two animals gives other examples of equivalent sets of two. Sets of three occur in many stories, rhymes and songs suitable for nursery children e.g. *Goldilocks and the Three Bears, Three Blind Mice,* the *Three Wise Men* at Christmas etc. and the children can again recognize that here are sets with the same number of members: the same number of members in fact as there are wheels on their tricycles or legs on the little stools in the reading corner.

Ordering
Ordering or seriation is the third of these activities so vital to number which can be experienced in the nursery school and then formalized in the infants. Through concrete experiences of ordering, the child will proceed to the ordering of numerals i.e. to ordinal numbers; first, second, third etc. There are many simple ordering toys that could be provided in the nursery school. Nesting beakers that can be fitted one inside the other or built into a pyramid of graduated sizes or sets of coloured wooden discs that can be fitted on to sticks in order of size: one excellent set of these has recently come on the market consisting of a wooden box containing discs of graduated sizes in each of four

Fig 2.11

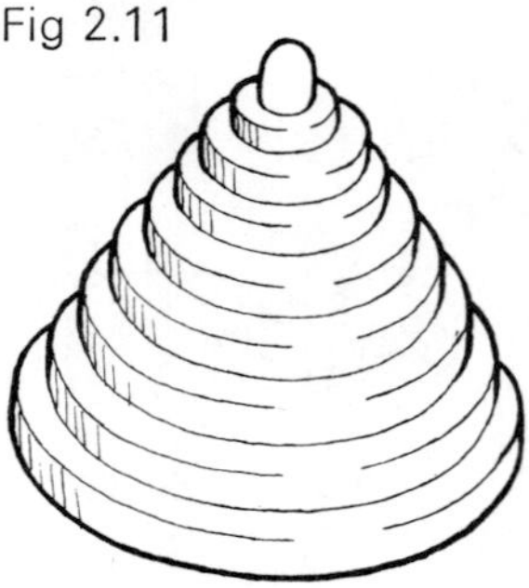

bright colours; red, blue, green and yellow, a set of pegs which will fit into any disc and a simple die marked on four faces with the four colours and blank on the other two. This set can be used for sorting according to colour, sorting according to size, ordering according to size in one colour, ordering according to size irrespective of colour and for games involving the die. As any disc can be used as a base, the discs can be ordered a few at a time by the less able, in size graduating from biggest to smallest or from smallest to biggest (see Fig 2.11). Any toy of the Billy Barrel type (barrels that unscrew at the centre to make pairs of cups in graduated sizes so that each contains another until the smallest contains a little man i.e. Billy) or the Russian Baboushka dolls provide more chances to put together in order, arrange in rows in order of size etc.

As well as toys constructed in this way there are many natural orderings in the nursery class environment. In the wendy house or home corner there will be saucepans and their lids in various sizes, dolls in various sizes with clothes in graduated sizes and beds of appropriate sizes. Building apparatus will provide bricks that can be arranged in order of size. The buildings made by the children can be ordered e.g towers of bricks, snakes or trains of bricks. Constructional toys can be used in the same way and the lengths of Lego or Meccano sorted according to length and ordered. Cuisenaire and Stern apparatus again give opportunities for ordering as do buttons or beads that can be ordered for size but can also be threaded on to strings and then ordered according to the length of string.

The children themselves can be ordered for height when waiting to go into the hall for movement and they can be encouraged to draw pictures showing orderings e.g. their families in order of size. A small group can be ordered as to who can throw a beanbag furthest or who can hop the longest etc. They can be encouraged to order pencils, crayons and paint brushes not just according to length but according to thickness or the width of the marks they make on paper. Pieces of paper can also be ordered for size; this ordering will be that of area if each successively smaller sheet fits inside the area of the last or by length or by width alone.

There are some very good ordering jigsaws available for small children. Here the same shape is repeated in decreasing sizes and each shape fits into an indentation on a board (see Fig 2.12). These

Fig 2.12

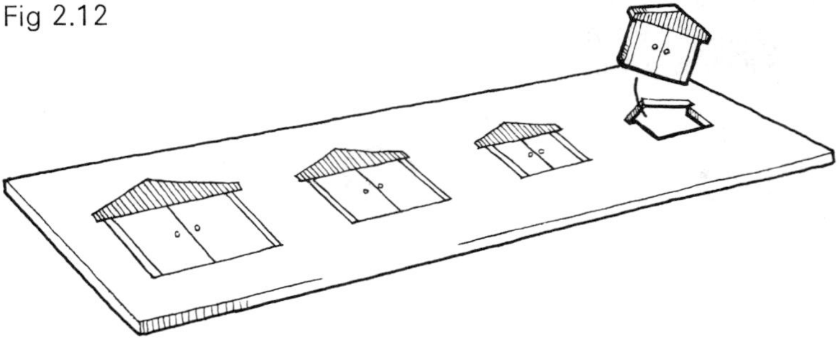

jigsaws are made in pairs so that the shapes from one board fit with those of another, e.g. one is a set of doll's prams and its partner consists of a set of small girls. Each cut-out will stand up on its own and so the girls can be matched to the prams and used for imaginative play (see Fig 2.13). More complicated ordering jigsaws are also on the

Fig 2.13

market which again consist of graduated cut-outs (by far the most suitable jigsaw for this age group) not just of one shape but of series of houses or trees etc. which form a picture.

Many stories, songs and rhymes provide opportunities for ordering and by involving the children in the making of friezes to illustrate these or the drawing of pictures or making of collages they become physically involved in the ordering. Again, *Goldilocks and the Three Bears* is one of the most useful as here we not only have the bears to order but the chairs, beds, porridge bowls, spoons and the amounts of porridge suitable for each bear.

In the infant school children will be involved in making sequential patterns to help with ordering. Some of these are simple enough to try with the brighter nursery child who needs enrichment activities. Very simple patterns involving two shapes, two colours or two sizes are suitable (see Fig 2.14). These the child must copy (a matching exercise) and continue. At this stage the copying will probably not be by drawing but by the actual putting out of counters or three-dimensional shapes that correspond to the ones put out by the adult.

Fig 2.14

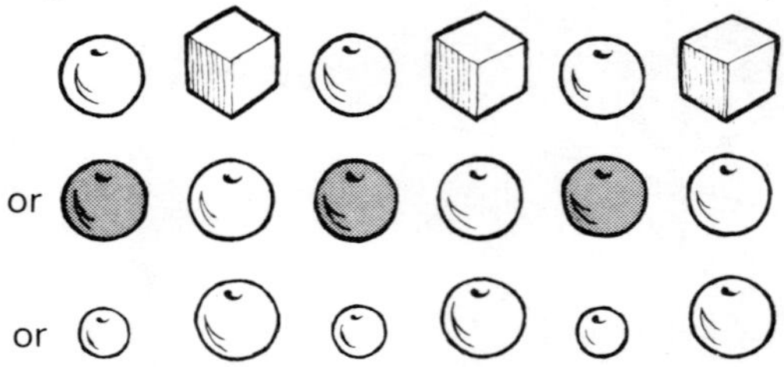

Sequential bead patterns can also be attempted so long as they are very simple ones. Bead threading is easy for this age child if he is provided with plastic threads and beads with good sized holes. Again, he will need beads not only of differing sizes and colours but of differing shapes.

Mathematical vocabulary

These three activities form the main part of the pre-number experiences suitable for nursery children but the nursery teacher should be aware of other number work that will be introduced in the primary school and build in to the child's experiences, activities that will foreshadow these as and when the occasion arises. Perhaps the most essential preparation for the child is hearing the use of correct mathematical vocabulary by the teacher. There is no need for adults to feel that they must use simple, and often incorrect, words when they talk with young children. The child has to learn new words and he may as well learn the right words from the start. The teacher must not only use the correct word but she must also be careful that she uses words correctly. One word that is very often used incorrectly is 'half'. This word has a very precise mathematical meaning and should not be used unless it is meant. Yet how many times do we hear a parent or a teacher, after cutting an apple or breaking a bar of chocolate into two pieces, refer to these pieces as halves and even go on to say 'Give Mary the bigger half!' It is virtually impossible to cut an apple into halves i.e. two exactly equal parts, or to break a bar of chocolate into halves. On the other hand we can give young children experience of the correct meaning of the word half when they are encouraged to fold a piece of paper into two equal pieces or when they are playing with mosaics and discover that two of the right-angled isosceles triangles fit together to make a square (see Fig 2.15). On these

Fig 2.15

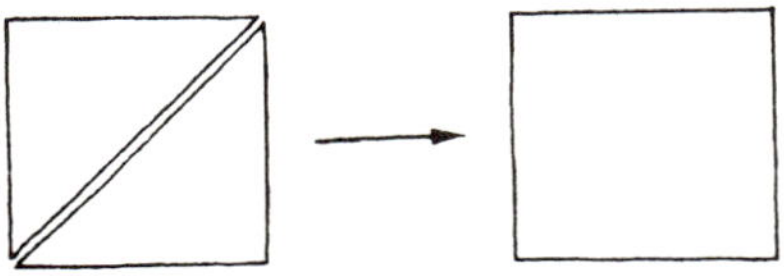

occasions the teacher can correctly use the word half. We can also give practical experiences to young children of the mathematical operations they will meet later on. For instance, the operation of addition. Nursery children can experience this within their play situations. When building a wall or a tower they will fetch a set of bricks and then, to make it larger or higher, will add to that set another set. At the water trough they may pour the contents of a yoghurt carton and then the contents of a cup into a large jug and so combine the two quantities or, when filling a bucket with damp sand to make a sandcastle they will add spadefuls of sand together. In teacher-led activities like baking, they will put three cupfuls of flour into a bowl and add three tablespoons of sugar etc. to make cakes or biscuits. They can be encouraged to add more beads to those already on a plastic thread or to lengthen their train of bricks by adding more bricks. These activities are all concrete examples of addition that will help children with the manipulation of abstract figures later on.

Other number experiences

Through some of these activities the young child will also gain experiences of the commutative property of addition. When he threads four blue beads and then three red ones on to his plastic thread, the teacher can encourage him to make another chain using three red beads first and then four blue ones. By matching the two chains he can discover from a concrete situation that the order of addition does not matter. In the junior school when faced with an addition such as $3+29$, if he has realized that the order of addition is immaterial, he will start with 29 and add on 3 rather than adding 29 on to 3.

In our discussion of matching we have already looked at one aspect of subtraction i.e. 'finding the difference'. The other two aspects, 'take away' and 'add on' can also be introduced through activities. 'Take away' involves the removal of a subset from a set. This is illustrated by five children playing in the wendy house and two deciding to go and play elsewhere. When a child pours away part of the contents of a jug, drinks some of the milk from a glass or eats some of a batch of cakes he is again experiencing the 'take away' situation. Some games can also illustrate this e.g. the knocking down of skittles (one of the cheapest sets of skittles is a collection of empty bleach bottles, well washed, and a plastic gamester type ball). The infant child would be encouraged to record the knocking down of two skittles out of a set of four as $4-2\rightarrow 2$ whereas the nursery child should be encouraged to verbalize what has happened (see Fig 2.16). Many number rhymes or

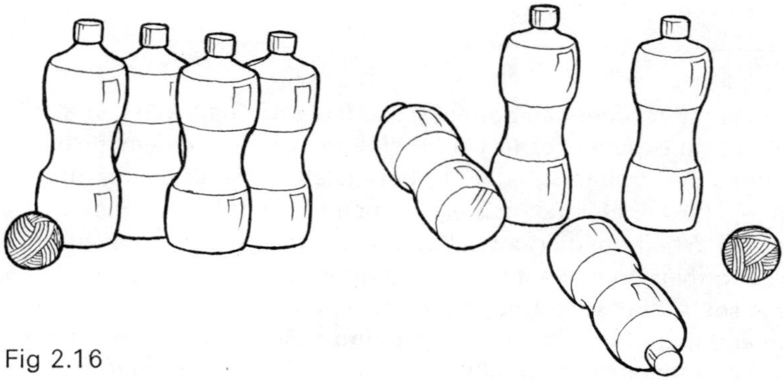

Fig 2.16

songs also give experience of this e.g. *Five little ducks went out to play*, *Ten Green Bottles* (which can always be simplified into five or six green bottles for the very young), or any rhyme or song where the members of the set are being removed one at a time, and, at this stage, are being acted out physically as they are sung or chanted.

The third aspect of subtraction is the one used everyday in shopping situations. The assistant in the chain store when given 50p to pay for an article costing 43p does not mentally take 43p away from 50p or match 43p with members of the set of 50p and find she has 7p unmatched. She adds on as she puts the change into the customer's hand. Experience of this can come from putting more beads on to a string to match the length of another string, adding more bricks to a tower to make it the same height as another or adding more carriages on to a train to make it the same length as another (see Fig 2.17). Another type of activity that gives the same sort of experience is pouring more orange squash into a glass to make it as full as another (see Fig 2.18), or shovelling more sand into a bucket to make it as full as the others.

Experiences towards multiplication were mentioned with regard to equivalent sets but to these we could add going upstairs two at a time, jumping or hopping over two squares in hopscotch type games. The two aspects of division can also be practically introduced. Division by partitioning (i.e. how many sets of 2 in a set of 6, or $6\div 2$?) can be experienced by seeing how many cups we can fill one at a time from this jug. At this stage the answer may well be 'that

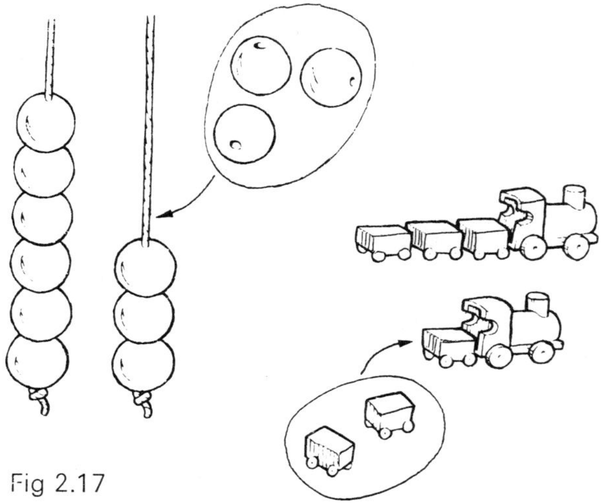

Fig 2.17

Fig 2.18

Fig 2.19

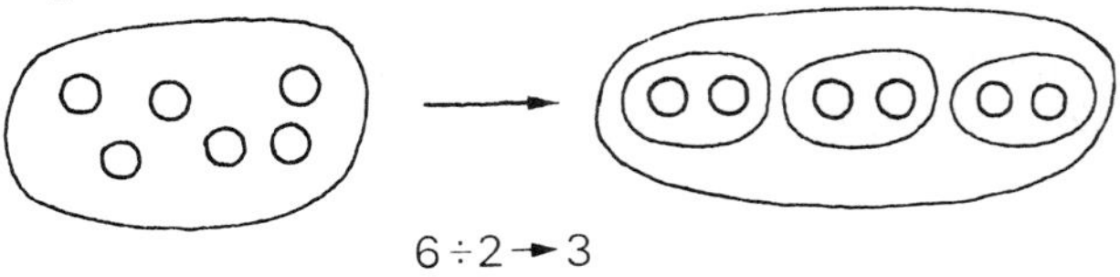

many' rather than a number (see Fig 2.19). During a dolls' tea party the child could be involved in seeing how many of the dolls sat round the table. Can each be given two cakes? Or, when helping with giving out equipment in movement sessions, he can be asked to take a box of beanbags and see how many children can each be given 2 bags. The other aspect of division, that of sharing (i.e. sharing a set of 6 among 3, or 6÷3) can be practised by the actual sharing out of the results of baking (see Fig 2.20) : one for Mary, one for Sue, one for Harry;

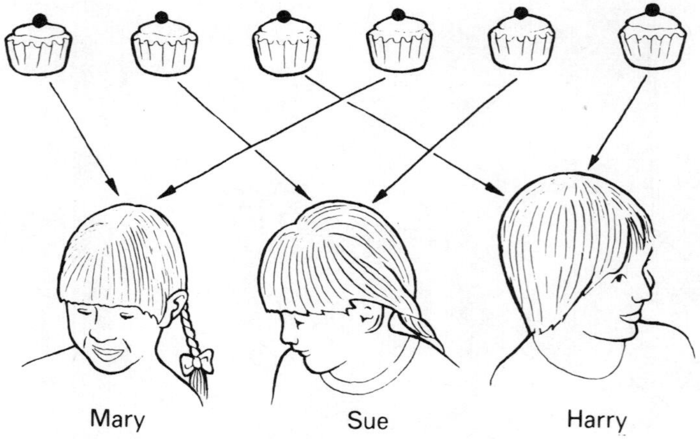

Fig 2.20

another for Mary, another for Sue, another for Harry, or by sharing the liquid in a jug between three glasses (note the difference between this and the partitioning example above: here we are not filling one glass and then going on to another glass, but endeavouring to share the liquid evenly among a number of glasses).

Summary

I have tried in this chapter to explain and give examples of the type of pre-number work that could be suitable in the nursery situation. Of course a teacher would not attempt to do all of this pre-number work with all of the children. But she must be aware of the pre-number possibilities, observe as they come up naturally in the children's play, watch how the individual copes with these situations and intervene if she feels it advantageous. Intervention could mean just putting down beside an engrossed child a further handful of beads or another container by the water trough; it could mean asking a question or it could mean making a suggestion or giving advice.

3

Measurement

To most people measurement means finding the length of a journey or the height of a building but we measure many other properties e.g. weight (or mass), area, volume, capacity, cost ,time, temperature, speed, angles, pressure, sound, density etc. Some of these are more suitable types of measurement than others for the young child but most of them will be used loosely in his conversation although not clearly understood. The teacher should recognize the difference between length which is a continuous quantity and number which is discontinuous. We use numbers, however, to measure length by means of some type of representation e.g. our desk may measure six handspans in length. Measures also refer to properties found in real situations e.g. the length of the room or the angle of elevation of the top of a tower, whereas numbers can be completely abstract (see Fig

Fig 3.1

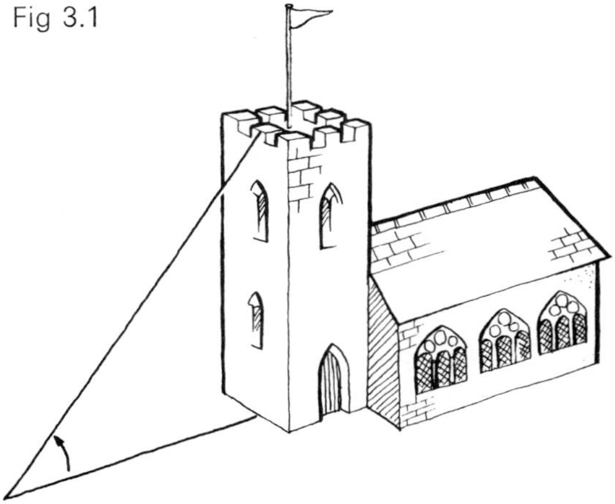

angle of elevation

3.1). The young child's first interest in size of any kind arises through contrasts e.g. 'I'm bigger than you', 'This bucket is heavier than that one', 'My tower is taller than yours.' Often these contrasts occur in the children's favourite stories such as *Jack and the Beanstalk, Goldilocks and the Three Bears, The Gingerbread Man.* From discussions of stories like these we can provide experiences for young children which will stimulate them to make judgements about these contrasts. In doing this the children are looking for relationships between things i.e. they are experiencing the study of relationships which is the essence of mathematics.

Length

The simplest type of measurement is that of length since it can be easily seen. Two different lengths of coloured string can be put side by side and it is immediately obvious that one is longer than the other. With all other types of measurement either an instrument is needed to test the relationship e.g. weight (or mass) where some type of scale pan is necessary, or time where some type of clock, no matter how primitive, must be used. Or the measurement involves more than one relationship e.g. area where it is necessary to look at both the length and the width and to realize that the longest shape does not always cover the greatest area, or volume where width, length and height are involved and the tallest article does not necessarily have the biggest volume.

Vocabulary

In the nursery class plenty of opportunities must be provided for children to compare lengths and for discussion amongst the children and with the teacher. It is through this discussion that the child's measurement vocabulary can be enlarged. Through imitating the teacher and other adults the child should be encouraged to use the correct vocabulary. At the same time the adult should be ready to welcome and accept the child's statements since remarks that sound strange or incorrect to us will probably be consistent with the child's stage of development e.g. 'I've got miles and miles of string.' Here the child is imitating his elders using the word mile to represent a long distance but his experience is such that, as yet, anything longer than familiar everyday things comes into the same category and is beyond his comprehension. This can be compared with the child's use of 'millions' when his recognition of numbers as small as seven is still insecure. He is enjoying these words for their own sake and for the sense of importance their use gives him without necessarily understanding them.

The teacher must encourage and increase the child's use of pre-measurement vocabulary such as 'bigger than', 'smaller than', 'about the same size as'. These words will be used intuitively at first and the child's reasons for bigness should be appreciated e.g. 'My bike is bigger than yours because it has three wheels.' Here either the idea of overall size has been muddled with the number of wheels or the remark is made as an unconscious compensation for the fact that the child's bike really does look smaller and he knows it! Other pre-measurement comparisons the child will use are:

longer than, shorter than, about the same length as
taller than, shorter than, about the same height as

(Notice the use of the same word 'shorter' for these two types of measurement which will be confusing to some children.)

wider than, narrower than, about as wide (narrow) as
fatter than, thinner than, about as fat (thin) as

(How often the young child confuses thin and narrow and refers to a 'thin' road. At this stage the teacher can accept the child's word but use the correct one herself.)

deeper than, shallower than, about as deep (shallow) as
far, near, about as far (near) as
higher than, lower than, about as high (low) as

Here is another point of confusion for many young children, the difference between taller than and higher than. Plenty of opportunities for the correct use of these words should be taken by the teacher. References can be made to heights of towers of bricks or the children themselves and the difference between these and the positions of children on rungs of the climbing frame, or books on different shelves made clear.

Comparisons of size
Opportunities for the use of these contrasting pre-measurement words will arise in the natural environment of the nursery classroom. The children themselves, the children and their teacher, the children and the classroom furniture will provide many of these. Their heights can be compared, the lengths of their shadows, lengths of their feet, how long their hair is, who has the largest stride and who has the biggest fathom i.e. the distance between their far thumbs (see Fig 3.2). Why this

Fig 3.2

distance between far-thumbs

particular body measurement has been used as a measure of sea depth always intrigued me until a student who had spent two years in the Merchant Navy prior to college explained that as you hauled upon rope from the sea you stretched your arms wide and so could count how many far-thumbs long it was! The children's clothes can also be compared; who is wearing long/short socks today, who has long trousers on, who has long/short sleeves, whose scarf is the longest and so on. The same types of comparisons can be made using the children's dolls and here we can add comparisons of fatness and thinness without personal offence.

The dressing-up box will provide shoes and hats that make the wearer taller or bulky coats that make them fatter. Some clothes will be too big or too long for the child and this will be discussed among the children. Another rich source of length comparisons is the wendy house. Here the beds can be compared in length and width, the bedding can be measured against the beds, the tabletop can be seen to be higher than the seats of the chairs, the handles of the saucepans will be of different lengths, some of the cleaning brushes will be long-handled and some short-handled, the curtains will be the same length as each other and the mats on the floor will be of differing lengths. Constructional toys will provide measuring activities both in the contents of the sets themselves and in the various towers, snakes, trains and models that will be made from them. Playdough and plasticine can also be made into models that can be compared for height or length. When painting or drawing, the thickness of the pencils, crayons or brushes can be discussed and the marks they make on paper compared for thickness or narrowness. The paper or card used will also vary in thickness and different sized pieces of paper should be available so that sometimes a child can choose a big piece and sometimes a smaller piece. The design, patterns and pictures that are produced will also provide comparisons. Discussions about depth and shallowness of water will occur at the water trough and the paddling pool and the depth of holes dug in the sandpit can be compared.

In music and movement sessions many of the suggestions made by the teacher will involve comparisons of size e.g. 'Curl up as small as you can, let's see who is the smallest', 'Now stretch up tall, taller still', 'Who can stretch themselves into the widest shape?', 'Who can make themselves the thinnest?' The musical instruments will also provide comparisons; the big drums and the smaller ones, the lengths of the drumsticks, the size of the heads of the sticks, the lengths of the strips on the xylophone. The same comparison words will be used about musical notes e.g. high and low (a difficult concept for the very young child). Loud and soft sounds will provide the beginnings of the measurement of sound.

Conservation of length
At intervals throughout the nursery stage the teacher should check whether or not children appreciate the conservation of length i.e. that the length of an article remains the same when that article is moved about. This links with the child's awareness of the constancy of objects mentioned in the first chapter. He will gradually become aware that an object remains the same despite its apparent change of size or shape when he views it from different positions. Appreciation of the constancy of length can be tested by showing the child two building bricks or pencils that are of the same length side by side and discussing their length with him. Then one of the building bricks should be moved slightly (see Fig 3.3), and the lengths of the two

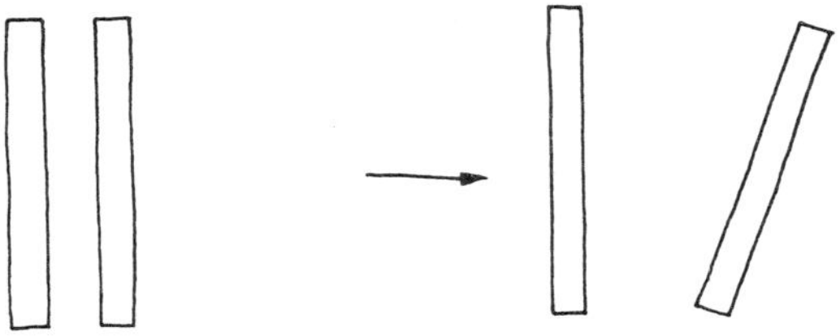

Fig 3.3

discussed again. At the pre-school stage many children will think that the brick that has been moved is now shorter than the other i.e. they do not appreciate that lengths remain the same when moved. If children are at this stage, the straight-forward comparison of lengths that can be put side by side is as much as they can understand and they are definitely not ready to use a representation, i.e. a measure, no matter how simple, for length. The discussion between the teacher and the child, and sometimes with other children, will help the child to grasp the concept of conservation but he will not always be secure in his understanding and his appreciation may lapse now and then and have to be reinforced by more discussion and practical comparisons. This is an example of what Piaget meant by our ability to accelerate a child's learning by providing suitable experiences.

Ordering by length
In the previous chapter when discussing order, it was suggested that children could be encouraged to order according to length. This is an extension of simple comparison in that it involves comparisons between more than two objects. As the child does this the teacher will be able to introduce the correct use of superlatives i.e. shortest and longest. The children can also be helped to make collections of tall (or long) things. These can be physical collections resulting in a 'tall corner' or can be cuttings from magazines of pictures of things

they know to be tall or they can be their own drawings of these things. These can be collected together on charts or in 'books'. As children do this they will probably discuss and argue over some object which one child thinks is tall but others do not. It is here that the idea of a measure can be simply introduced. The children need something to measure against and the obvious thing for them to use is themselves. Their collection of tall things becomes a collection of things 'taller than us' and so teacher goes into the collection along with the giraffe and the windowpole. Similar collections can be made of things shorter than us. If the teacher feels that the children's idea of length is established firmly enough she can build on this and suggest that the children now imagine themselves to be elephants and see if they can think of things that will be tall to the elephant and then small to the elephant. The children may realize that teacher and the windowpole, both of which were 'taller than us', now go into the set of things smaller than an elephant. This could be the beginnings of their realization that all measurement is relative i.e. it depends what you are comparing with or what you use as a measure. The same sort of imaginative game can be played using an ant or a fly so that the children again see that things such as the daisies in the school grass which are small to them, are, in fact, tall to an ant or a fly. These experiences of collecting tall things and the relativeness of measurement will be repeated in the infant school and formalized.

Measures

These two steps, the straightforward comparison of objects put side by side and the use of the children themselves as measures, are the first steps in the teaching of measurement which apply to most of the aspects of measurement listed at the beginning of this chapter. The nursery teacher should understand the rest of this development although some of it will not be suitable for the children in her care. After the comparison stage and the resultant need for a measure, will come the necessity to answer the question 'How much taller?' i.e. smaller measures are needed. It is at this stage that the infant teacher will encourage the use of body measurements, i.e. will encourage the children to follow the development of early man who used what he always had with him, his body, as a measuring system. Infant children will use their footlengths, handspans, paces, thumb widths, hand widths, yards (tip of nose to tip of finger), fathoms, cubits (elbow to tip of fingers) etc (see Fig 3.4). This is usually referred to as the stage of arbitrary measures and along with the body measures the children can use anything they have plenty of in the classroom e.g. straw lengths, new pencil lengths, ruler lengths, cuisenaire orange rod lengths etc. This is a most useful stage in the teaching of measurement because so many important steps can be incorporated within it. The first is how

Fig 3.4

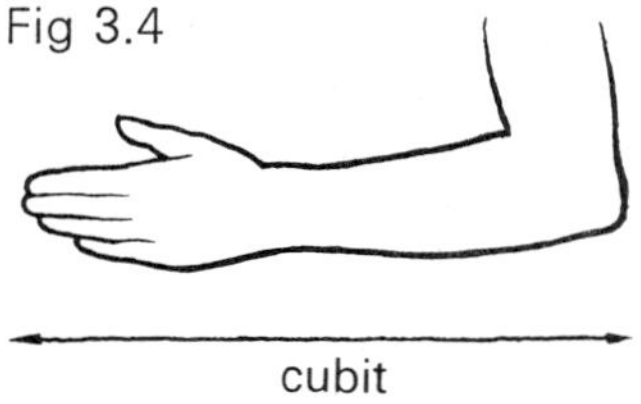

to use a measure. So many teachers take it for granted that the young child will know how to use a ruler and yet are not surprised that they themselves need to be shown how to use measuring devices such as micrometers. The ruler is just as difficult for some young children. It is easier to help a child with the use of a measure if he has more than one i.e. it is best to use a handful of straws to find his friend's height than to use just one. By getting his friend to lie down on the floor he can then put straws end to end along his friend's length (notice how this ties up with the constancy of length, his friend's height being the same as his length) and both he and his friend can see that his length is six and a bit straws (see Fig 3.5). This fitting of the straws end to end helps with the use of a measure and the putting out of a succession of straws helps with the counting.

Fig 3.5

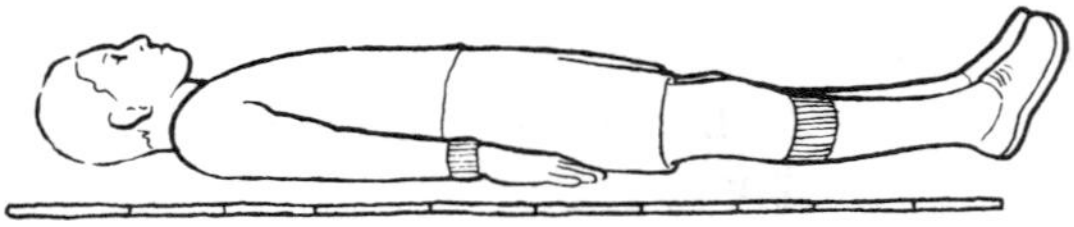

Children should also be encouraged to estimate (not guess) how long an article is before it is measured. This can be begun in the nursery school by getting the children to look carefully at articles and to say which they think will be the longer, or the shorter, before they put them side by side to compare. This will help them gradually to realize that an object looks smaller than it really is when it is at a distance. After the practical measurement has been done, the infant child will record his results and here the importance of stating units will be stressed. It would be no good recording 'My friend's length is six and a bit', we must know what was used as a measure. The suitability of measures will also be discussed i.e. if we are measuring the width of Jane's birthday cards, thumb widths would be suitable but if we are measuring the length of the corridor we would use a bigger unit of length, probably a pace.

Standard measures

After this stage of arbitrary measures the infant children will be led to realize that they need a standard measure. Mary might have measured the corridor outside the classroom and found it was 28 of her paces but John found it was 25 of his. This often results in discussions as to whether one of them has done it wrongly or lost count and the teacher will help them to see that both of them were probably right but that their paces differ. Then it is interesting to listen to the children's discussions as to whose pace is the longer. Many infant children will say that Mary's pace is the longer because she had the bigger result and it will not be until the two children have paced side by side that they will see that, in fact, it is John who has the bigger pace. By trying to describe their school to someone who has never seen it, the children can be led to realize that their body measurements will mean nothing to someone who does not know them and so we must all use a measure that is understood by everyone. It is now possible to introduce the metre and centimetre although care must be taken when measuring in centimetres that the resulting number of centimetres are within the children's understanding i.e. if the children are having difficulty in understanding tens and units, measurements of 69 cm will be meaningless to them. The question of accuracy should also be discussed with the children so that they realize that, for different purposes, different standards of accuracy are needed. If we are measuring a journey we rarely use anything more accurate than so many miles (kilometres soon) or so many miles and a half, but if we were an architect designing a house we would need to be far more accurate and an engineer needs to be more accurate still. These main stages in the teaching of length can be applied to most other aspects of measurement which can all be begun in the nursery school.

Weight

Weight (or mass) is a much more difficult concept than length. It cannot be seen, the larger article will not always weigh the most and it cannot always be felt correctly by comparing the weight of things in our hands. A small, concentrated, weight will feel much heavier than the same weight that is distributed over a larger area. To test this, try weighing a 16 oz packet of cornflakes in one hand and a one pound weight in the other. Although you will know that they are equal in weight the one pound weight will still feel much heavier than the cornflakes! In order to compare weights, then, the nursery child will need to use simple balance pans. At this stage a lot of free play should be allowed, just simply letting the children put things into the pans and watch the pans go up and down. As the children do this the teacher should ask why they think one pan is going down while the other goes up to see if they understand the use of this very simple machine; again, the understanding of the machine, like the use of a ruler, should not be taken for granted. Play in the grounds of the school on a seesaw will probably help with this understanding and the teacher should encourage the children to see the connection between the seesaw and the simple balance pans.

Plenty of opportunities for weighing all sorts of materials and objects should be provided in the nursery so that comparisons can be made. Measures, i.e. standard weights, should not be used at this stage but the children should be encouraged to compare the weights of anything and everything that will go into the scale-pans and discuss results. They can again attempt estimations so that they challenge themselves to see if they are correct in thinking that the toy engine is heavier than the lorry. Simple 'cooking' can be introduced at this stage although the recipes should involve cupfuls or spoonfuls rather than ounces or grammes. Ingredients can be weighed against each other too e.g. the same weight of flour as an egg. The difference in the weight of the ingredients before and after cooking can be discussed by finding something that weighs about the same as the ingredients before they are cooked and weighing the cooked buns against that same article. The children's reasons for the difference in weight are often very interesting and, again, will tell the teacher a great deal about the stage of the child's understanding and thought processes. Often the reasons given are completely wrong but surprisingly logical.

Conservation of mass

Just as we test the child's understanding of the conservation of length so we should test his understanding of the conservation of mass. This can be done as the child investigates and compares weights of plasticine or playdough. He can find something that balances his block of plasticine and then be encouraged to roll the plasticine out into a long, thin, snake. Often he will think that the snake will weigh much more than the original block of plasticine because it is longer and will be surprised to find that it is, in fact, exactly the same weight. Now, if he breaks the snake into lots of pieces and rolls them into little balls he will be unsure whether this collection will weigh more or less than the original block or the long snake. He needs help, through experiences such as these, to realize that the mass of something remains the same even though it takes different shapes provided nothing is lost in the shaping and nothing is added. This can be linked with the problem of the cooked buns and the question asked, 'Has anything been lost in the cooking?'

Experiences of weight will also be gained as children play, especially as they play outdoors. They will try to carry buckets of sand or water and will find some 'too heavy to carry'. Some children will leave those that are too heavy and try to find a lighter one but others will tip out some of the sand or water to make the bucket lighter in weight. If it is appropriate, i.e. does not interfere with or stop a child's imaginative play, the teacher could ask why the child did this. At this early age he may have tipped out the sand intuitively and not be able to say why or he may have done it as a conscious act to lighten the load of the sand. These intuitive or conscious acts tell us a great deal about his thought processes and understanding of measurement. Children love pushing or pulling each other in go-carts, trolleys or pushchairs. Whilst doing this they will comment that Jane is heavier to push than Tom, that they cannot push Jane and Mary together because they are too heavy and so one must get out of the truck. As they tidy away building bricks etc. they will pile them into boxes and may find these boxes too heavy to lift. They will discuss amongst themselves that the box of plastic bricks is easier to lift than the wooden ones. Re-arranging furniture in the wendy house or in the classroom itself will also provide experiences of weight and opportunities for discussion.

Area

As far as area is concerned, the most important contribution at this stage is to help the children understand what is meant by the term. In many adult minds the word 'area' immediately produces the response 'length times breadth' and yet this formula for finding area only applies when calculating the area of a rectangle or of a shape dependent in some way on rectangles (see Fig 3.6). The nursery teacher

Fig 3.6

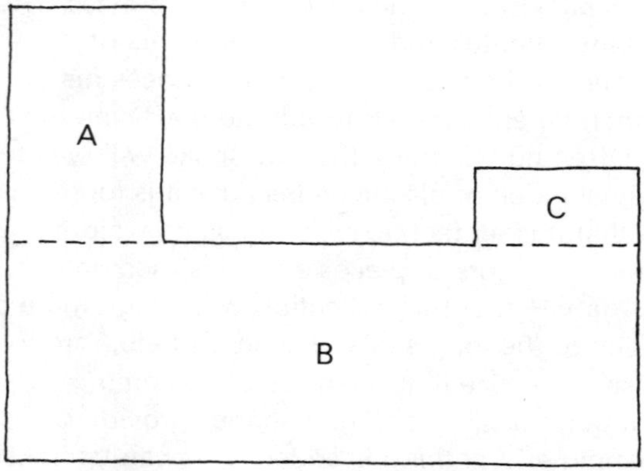

total area = area A + area B + area C

should use the word naturally in everyday situations so that the children become familiar with it and intuitively begin to understand its meaning. Various sections of the classroom will be allocated for different purposes and these can be referred to as 'the carpeted area', the 'quiet area' etc. When painting models the children can be encouraged to paint 'the whole area' a chosen colour and the painting of friezes can also be used as an opportunity to refer to area in a meaningful way. In the playground reference can be made to 'the grass area' or 'the hard area' and in movement sessions the children can be asked to use 'the whole area' of floor space as they run, hop etc. Many of their play activities will involve comparisons of areas e.g. fitting sheets and blankets to dolls' beds, seeing that some sheets are too small for one bed but fit the baby's cot, putting a tablecloth on the table in the wendy house, laying new fitted carpets in the dolls' house, covering tables with sheets of polythene or newspaper before modelling in clay or painting, seeing that some baking trays will fit into the oven while others are too big etc. Ironing of dolls' clothes will give another type of area experience.

Shapes
An introduction to the way in which area can be measured will come from playing with brightly coloured floor mosaics or gummed shapes and finding that some shapes will tessellate e.g. squares, rectangles, equilateral triangles, hexagons, while others will not e.g. pentagons, octagons (see Fig 3.7). From trying to fit some of these shapes together

Fig 3.7

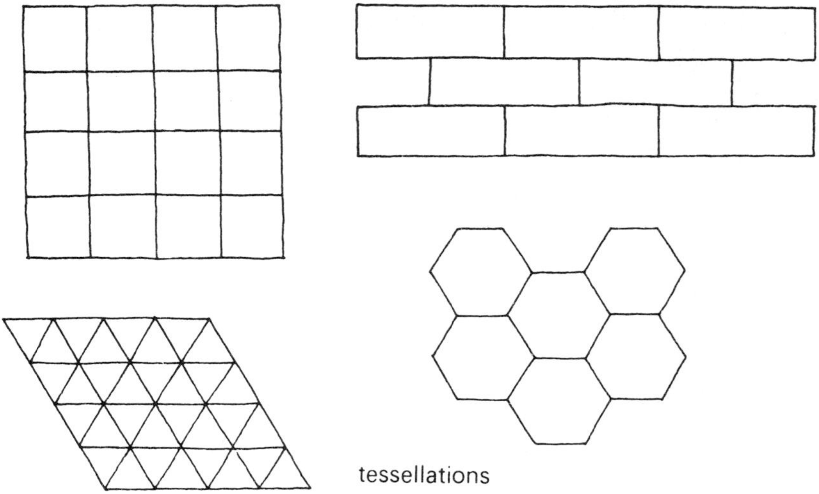

tessellations

the children may realize for themselves that squares are by far the easiest shapes to fit together and so are naturally used as measures of area. The children's individual mats that some nurseries use for movement or the rugs used at storytime can also be fitted together and the tessellating

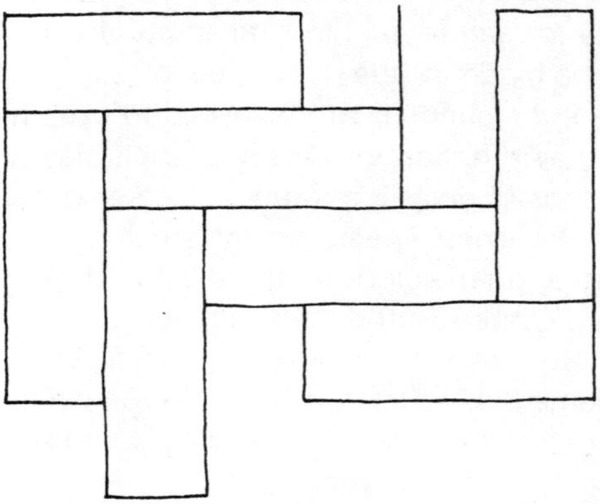

Fig 3.8

patterns on parquet flooring or brick walls appreciated (see Fig 3.8). Making different patterns using the same collection of shapes will provide an initial experience in the conservation of area. This will be stressed in the junior school but very young children can play with tangrams and produce pictures or patterns all having the same area. A tangram is an old Chinese pastime and one of the simplest is a square cut up and then arranged in many different ways with all the rearrangements having the same area as the original square (see Fig 3.9).

Fig 3.9

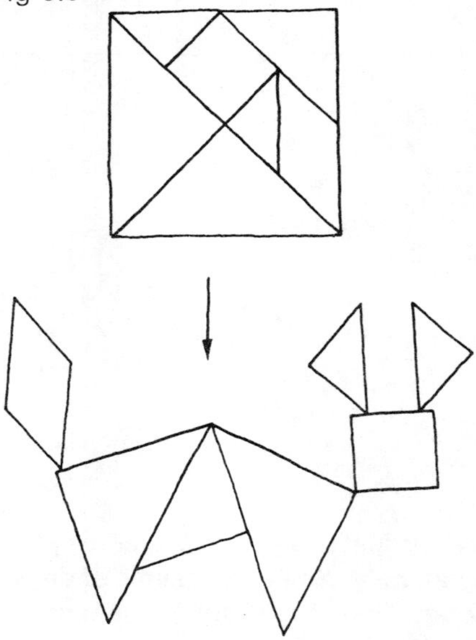

Volume and capacity
The understanding of volume and capacity can also begin in the nursery school. Capacity is the measurement of what will go into a container whereas volume is the measurement of the material from which an object is made. These are often confused even in adult minds because to help us picture volume we sometimes think of the object as hollow and discuss what would be needed to fill it. Water and sandplay will involve children in filling containers and comparing how much will go into jugs, buckets, cups etc. Again, we must not take it for granted that a child realizes that when he pours all the liquid from a jug into a bottle and the bottle is still not full, that the bottle must hold more than the jug (see Fig 3.10). He needs to be

Fig 3.10

encouraged to verbalize what has happened. Discussions about what we mean by full are also necessary and practice in careful pouring, using funnels, so that no liquid is lost as they try to compare capacity. Many different types of containers should be provided; tall and short, fat and thin, transparent and opaque, straight-sided and bulbous, with pouring lips and without, with handles and without and even sieves and colanders so that the children experience things that will hold water and those that do not. The number of containers provided at any one time will depend on the size of the water trough, pool, sandtray or sandpit. The teacher can plan the children's experiences by providing certain types of containers at different times. One day she might put out many different shaped containers which she knows all hold roughly the same amount. This would provide experiences of the conservation of capacity i.e. that the same amount of sand or liquid can take very different shapes; a concept that is difficult for many older children and even adults to appreciate. At other times the choice of containers could be left entirely to the children. Of course not only containers will be provided for these activities but spoons, forks, rakes, spades, sticks of different thicknesses, spatulas etc. will also be needed and these will again provide measurement discoveries and discussions.

Packing building bricks back into their boxes at the end of play, finding the right-sized box to put things into, putting toys away into wheeled storage trucks will all give valuable experiences of packing space. The children will discover that cubes and cuboids will fit into boxes more easily than some other shapes and so will be experiencing why we use cubes as measures of capacity and volume although many types of prisms and other three-dimensional shapes such as tetrahedrons will also stack together leaving no spaces in between and so could be used as measures. The fact that water is displaced when articles are immersed in it can be noticed and discussed. This will be extended later and used as a method of calculating volume when the children are older.

The school pets can also be useful here. They can be compared for size: tallest, shortest; smallest, biggest (in volume); longest, shortest; fattest, thinnest; length of tails and ears can be compared; sizes of spots or paws or eyes etc. The volume and weight of the food they eat can also be discussed. The weight of the food portions can be simply compared using the balance pans and the volume of the food either by measuring it out in yoghurt cartons-full, by counting if the numbers are small or comparing by matching if too many for their number appreciation, or by using a larger container and marking off the level of the hamster's food, using a chinagraph pen, and then the level of the guinea pig's and seeing which eats the most (see Fig 3.11).

Fig 3.11

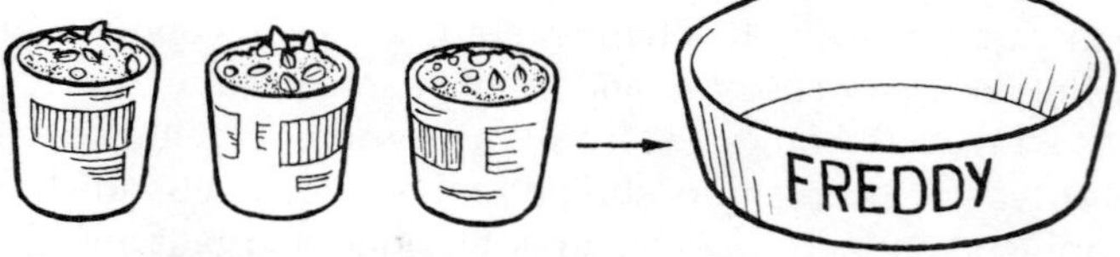

3 yoghurt cartonfuls for the hamster's feed

How much water they drink can be compared by giving them the same size water dishes and measuring the depth of water at specific times, probably using a dip-stick. This will also need discussion, the teacher being careful not to put words into the children's mouths but to encourage their verbalizations first and then use the correct words or better phrases for them to imitate if they wish.

Time

Time is a most difficult concept for young children as it cannot be seen, heard or felt by them and it even appears to pass at a different rate when they are happily engrossed in something they enjoy than when they are eagerly awaiting an expected treat or being made to do something they do not enjoy. Despite this, many very helpful experiences can be built into the nursery programme. There are two very different aspects of time; that of dial reading, or telling the time, and that of measuring the passing of time. Far too much emphasis is put on the first of these in many infant schools where the children spend hours drawing clock faces and trying to learn the hours, halfhours, five minutes, time past the hour and time to the hour. With many children this is a complete waste of precious time that could be spent on far more worthwhile activities as they lack the incentive to learn this. If, however, grandfather gives them a watch at Christmas, they can usually tell the time by the end of Boxing Day! It is experience in the measuring of the passing of time that they need at that stage and not the dial reading.

The passing of time

The nursery teacher will take every opportunity to refer to lengths of time e.g. 'We will have our story in about ten minutes' or 'It took you seven minutes to put the bricks away today John. Let's see if you can be quicker tomorrow' or 'We haven't got time for that today'. Simple timing devices can be taken into the nursery, discussed and used e.g. sandclocks of the egg-timer type. The children can talk about what is happening in the sandclock and might even make a very simple model of one using a cone-shaped plastic cup with a hole in the base fitted inside a jam jar and filled with cooking salt (see Fig 3.12). Use a

Fig 3.12

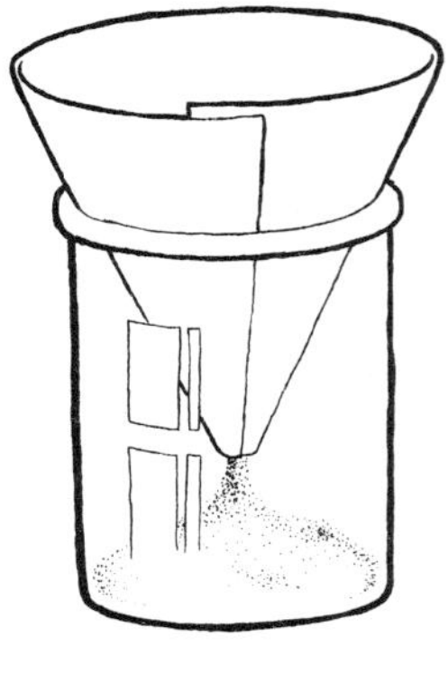

cone-shaped cup as it helps to direct the salt towards the hole and makes a better 'clock' than a flat based container. The hole should not be too small or the salt will take too long to pass through it and the children's interest will be lost, and must not be too big or the 'clock' will not last long enough. Salt is much better for this than sand as the bags of salt sold in grocer's shops have an additive to keep the salt dry whereas sand tends to get damp and clog up the hole in the cup. The egg-timer or home-made salt clock should be used to time all sorts of events in the nursery e.g. how long the hamster takes to eat his food, how long it takes the children to change for a movement session, how long the story took, how long it took Susan to mop up the 'tea' spilled in the wendy house etc. A child will have to be put in charge of the clock and will have to 'count' how many times it has to be turned upside down or filled. This counting will be done by tallying or matching the operation with a counter or shell and then the shells matched with yesterday's timing shells etc.

Another home-made clock that young children enjoy is the Chinese alarm clock (see Fig 3.13). This was originally an ornate metal dragon with an incense stick along its back, metal weights hung over its back

Fig 3.13

Chinese alarm clock

and a gong under the dragon. The incense stick burned all night and when it burned through the thread connecting the metal weights they fell on to the gong and sounded the alarm. This can be easily copied by using a metal ruler or strip of some other non-burnable material kept above the table by a brick at either end. A joss stick is the best thing to use to burn along the metal strip as anything else tends to go out in this horizontal position. Two large glass beads or fishing weights can be hung over the joss sticks with nylon thread and a metal plate will act as the gong. The length of time before the alarm sounds can be adjusted by positioning the thread with the weights close to the burning end of the joss stick. Again, the time taken should not be too long if the children are waiting for the alarm. This can be used after the initial interest in just hearing the alarm has worn off, to indicate when it is time to pack away the toys and come and sit on the mats for a story or when it is time to go outside to play, by the teacher carefully judging the period of time and arranging the weights in the appropriate position.

The connection between time and the sun can be stressed by watching and commenting on the position of the sun, or by drawing round the shadow cast on the floor, by a cross or some other mark stuck on the window at various times of the day. The names of the days of the week must also be discussed and any particular activity that always happens on specific days. Once upon a time Monday was always washing day but with so many mothers out at work, Saturday or Sunday are far more likely to be washing days now. The children can be encouraged to draw or paint what happens on certain days e.g. Mrs Jones who comes in to play the piano for their dancing session on Tuesdays, and an illustrated week made. The seasons and special yearly events, not forgetting their own birthdays, can be discussed and illustrated in the same way. The growing of plants and bulbs will also help children with the idea of the passing of time.

Dial reading

Dial reading will begin by the teacher referring the children or individuals to the clock whenever the opportunity arises, 'Look, it's half-past ten, that means it's time for your milk.' What the clock face looks like should be discussed i.e. that it is round and has one long hand and one short one (measurement of length comparisons!) The children's attention should be drawn to where these hands are at important times like 'dinner-time' and 'home-time'. If possible, plastic clocks with moveable hands should be provided for the children to set themselves. These, again, can be home-made out of card with a brass paper fastener keeping the hands together but free to be moved independently. One of these clocks should be in the wendy house so that the children can be encouraged to set the time for the activity they are involved in e.g. 'tea-time' or 'baby's bed-time'. At this stage it does not matter very much if the setting of the clock is incorrect although the teacher might intervene and discuss what the clock ought to look like if she can do so without spoiling the make-believe or intruding on an engrossed child. Reference can be made to the clock when baking e.g. 'The cakes will be cooked when the bigger hand gets to here', or when it is time to feed pets.

Other Measures

The opportunity to make some reference or to discuss most of the other aspects of measurement listed at the beginning of this chapter will arise out of day to day happenings. Measurement of temperature will be anticipated by reference to the heat of the sun's rays through the window or to the cold wind outside. The heat of food and drink or water to wash in will also be commented on and when baking the temperature of the oven will be vital and the use of the regulo setting will have to be discussed. Both play situations and real happenings will provide these opportunities. The beginnings of measurement of angles will be discussed in the next chapter but will also be through straightforward comparison. Different speeds will be compared in many activities; speeds of running, talking, eating etc. All children will have some experience of measuring cost. Coin recognition can be encouraged and the price of various articles discussed. This experience with money will be most useful later on as many children who have difficulty with operations with abstract numbers can often cope if the problem is turned into one concerning money. This is a practical application of number that is used too little with children who appear to be backward with number work.

Summary

Within this chapter I have attempted to show how various aspects of measurement can be introduced in the nursery class; how most of these aspects begin with straightforward comparison using some simple measuring device for all except length which can be compared by eye. These early comparisons and the practical introduction to conservation will be extended in the infant school following, with most aspects, the same type of development as I have indicated for length.

4

Shape

Shape is a most important area of mathematics for young children. It is the branch of mathematics that used to be called geometry and was rarely introduced before the secondary school. At this stage it was highly abstract. Most adults remember this geometry as diagrams consisting of circles and lines drawn on the blackboard which meant precious little to them and which apparently had no practical application. Despite this they were expected to form hypotheses concerning these shapes and to draw logical conclusions about them. To a few members of their class these theorems and their applications to further abstract riders were fascinating and satisfying but to the majority they were something that had to be endured and learned by heart in order to pass an examination. Most of this geometry dealt with two-dimensional figures which were themselves completely abstract. The geometry that can be explored with young children deals with three-dimensional shapes i.e. the world in which they live. The older child can be led to a study of two-dimensional shapes by discussing the shapes of the faces of these three-dimensional ones. Children are surrounded by shapes of all types; they sit on shapes, they sleep on shapes, they eat off and drink out of shapes, they climb over and through shapes, they build with shapes etc. The everyday objects which surround the child will, then, provide many interesting shapes to be explored and discussed but further stimuli can be provided and, again, it is the building up of correct vocabulary that is so vital at this early stage.

Shapes in the nursery

Inside the nursery school many shapes should be available for the child to handle; boxes of building bricks of all shapes and sizes, colours and materials; large, brightly coloured floor mosaics; empty cartons, tins and containers of all types; unusually shaped off-cuts of wood; pieces of plastic drainpipe and guttering; different sized plastic or wooden beads and buttons; cotton reels and other junk materials. The children and their parents can help to build this collection and to replace it as it becomes tatty and dirty. Mothers can help supply interestingly shaped empty packets e.g. *Toblerone, J-cloth* and cheese cartons, and fathers can collect the carefully sandpapered off-cuts of wood and the building site materials. Larger, indoor toys should be chosen with shape work in mind too so that children have large open shapes to climb inside, wriggle through, climb over etc. In the playground more of this type of toy and the different shaped climbing frames will provide shapes to be used just for the joy of climbing up, over and in and out but also for imaginative play. The teacher should watch how these are used, which ones become boats or aeroplanes etc., and try to find out why these particular shapes have been chosen. Often the child's answers will tell her which of the properties of that shape the child has recognized in his own particular way but she must also be prepared for the child's answer to be simply, 'I don't know' or, 'Because I did', either because he does not know why he chose it, cannot express his reasons in words or because he does not want to be disturbed by this interfering adult!

As he uses these shapes the child is unconsciously sorting them according to their various attributes. When he builds he is unconsciously selecting shapes with flat faces that will rest easily on one another. A very young child does not do this, he just puts one shape on top of another and is either furious because those with curved faces roll off or delighted because they do fall off and make a noise as they roll away. I remember my own son before he could walk or even crawl, spending a lot of time building with the collection of 'toys' we had given him. Many of these were household containers such as a syrup tin with a couple of pebbles inside. He could control and balance quite a few shapes but, at one particular stage, did not realize that a curved surface would not easily balance on a flat one. As the curved tin rolled off, usually knocking the rest of his tower down, he would scream and drum his heels on the ground. This lasted about a week and then it seemed to slowly dawn on him why this was happening and he would carefully turn the tin round and triumphantly put the flat end on to the top of his tower instead of the curved side. He was certainly not able to verbalize what he had done but children in the nursery school should be encouraged and helped to do so.

Vocabulary and definitions

Prisms

If we look at a set of children's building bricks, almost all of them will be prisms of one sort or another. Many will be cuboids, cylinders or wedge shapes, all members of the prism family, but some will be pyramids (see Fig 4.1). At our level we can define a prism as a three-dimensional shape with congruent and parallel end faces whose

Fig 4.1

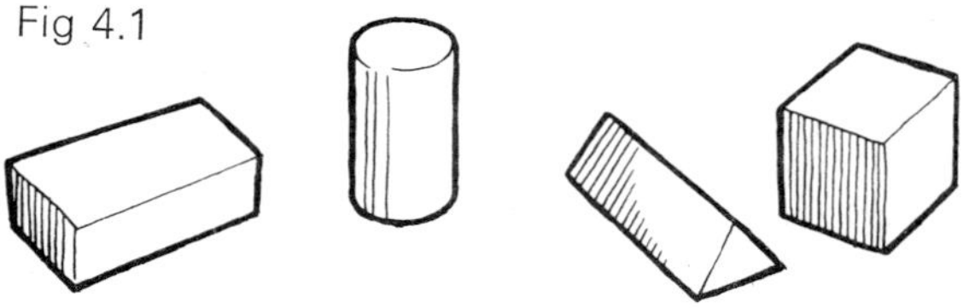

members of the prism family

cross-section parallel to those end faces is always congruent to them. This definition probably needs translating : congruent means exactly the same shape and size, parallel means keeping the same distance apart. Many of us will remember having learned that parallel planes were ones that never met. It is always better for young children to use a positive definition rather than a negative one like that. This definition of a prism is certainly too complex for many primary school children. The best child's definition of a prism that I have come across was given me by a girl of eight who suggested that prisms were packs of cards, all the same shape and size, piled on top of one another. Defined like this, she could imagine lifting off part of the pile of cards and seeing the constant cross section (see Fig 4.2). She then went on, with a little

Fig 4.2

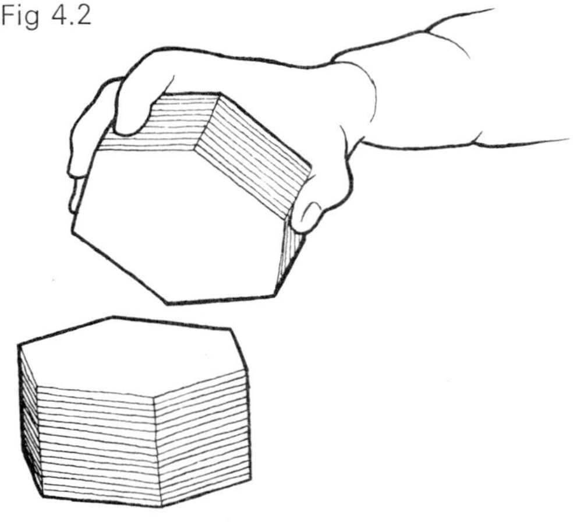

prompting, to use this definition to help her define a pyramid and called that a stack of similar cards i.e. cards that were all the same shape but not necessarily the same size, gradually getting smaller and smaller until the last one was only a dot. This is the type of child's definition which shows us that they have really thought about the shape and appreciated its properties. Obviously we cannot expect any such precise definition from nursery children but we can help them to progress towards it.

Cuboids

When a child builds he will choose mainly cuboids, partly because he intuitively recognizes that the flat surfaces will rest easily on one another, partly because his set of bricks has more cuboids in it than any other shape but also partly because he is unconsciously repeating the patterns around him in brick walls, tiled floors etc. Often it will be worthwhile to call the child's attention to these patterns and their similarity to the patterns he is making as he builds. He is also experiencing for himself the vital importance of the cuboid in our daily life. He is surrounded by furniture, houses etc. which are made up of cuboids or which have cuboids as part of them. The teacher should try as the opportunity arises to get the child to notice the use of the cuboid around him and to define this shape in his own words i.e. to express what it is that is vital to this shape and makes it different from others. As he tries to verbalize this the teacher will again accept his words but translate them into more correct language so that the child, by imitation and experience, begins to refer to faces, edges, rectangles, squares, right angles etc. Many teachers seem to feel that because they did not begin to learn about angles until the secondary school, right angles are too difficult a concept for young children and so refer to 'square corners' in a misguided effort to make them more easily understood. If a child is trying to express the idea of a right angle he should be helped to call it by its correct name and should not be taught something that will have to be unlearned later on. Define the right angle for the child as the vital property of the cuboid and link it correctly with the fact that the cuboid stands upright when placed on any of its faces. Encourage the child to feel a right angle so that when he feels the angles of the end faces of a triangular prism he will feel that some of these angles are sharper than the angles of the cuboid i.e. they are less than a right angle and so are called acute angles. Let him feel an obtuse angle and realize that this is an angle that is blunter, or not so sharp, as the angles of the cuboid ; in other words encourage the use of the angle of his cuboid as a measure i.e. something with which to compare other angles and so to make a beginning on the measurement of angles. Many teachers play a type of identification game with young children by giving them shapes to feel behind their backs or with their eyes shut so that they have to describe the shape by what it feels like.

As the child endeavours to put into words the other properties of the cuboid, the teacher can again help him to find other examples of these properties. The parallelism of the opposite faces can be found around him in the opposite edge of the table, the sides of the door frame, the window frames, the rungs of the climbing frame, the sections of the radiator, the bookshelves and the covers of the books themselves. He certainly does not need to go out of the classroom to the railway track in order to see examples of parallelism and yet most adults will remember this as the only example that they were given in their schooldays. The shapes of the faces of the cuboid can be identified as squares or rectangles and further examples of these found in the faces of other shapes or on the tiled floor, the tabletops, the books, the storage boxes and the windows. Many adults use the word oblong rather than the correct word rectangle. An oblong must have one pair of opposite sides longer than the other pair but a rectangle can have all its sides equal in length i.e. the set of squares is a subset of the set of rectangles (see Fig 4.3). When the child can count

Fig 4.3

i.e. can make a one–one correspondence between the number names and objects, he will be able to tell us that a cuboid has six faces; another vital property of this particular shape. He will probably be able to recognize the equality of the lengths of some of the edges of the cuboid and he will be able to find other equally sized cuboids by comparing building bricks for length, width and height. At first, if he is asked to find another 'the same size as this one' he may look at length only and the teacher may have to help him to realise that widths and heights must also be compared.

Pyramids

If we continue to observe the child building with his set of bricks we will see that he often chooses a pyramid to top off his tower i.e. one of the shapes that 'comes up to a point'. He will appreciate the different types of pyramid by noticing the different shapes of their bases and should be encouraged to talk about square-based pyramids or triangular based ones etc. and to realize that a pyramid with a circular base can also be called a cone although he may not recognize it as such until it is held up the other way (see Fig 4.4). He will also

Fig 4.4

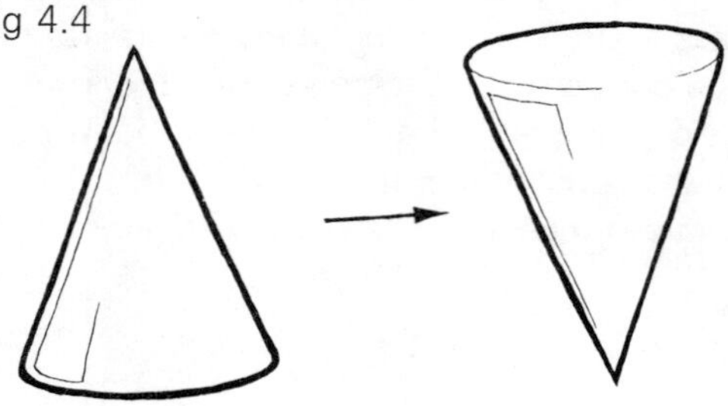

use three-dimensional shapes to build 'models' i.e. engines, houses, boats, rockets etc. As we watch him select a cylinder for the boiler of the engine or for the body of the rocket, we see that he is intuitively recognizing the properties of this shape. It is worth trying to discuss with him why he chooses the empty, circular, cheese packets for the wheels of his engine. When he tries to explain this he is attempting his first definition of a circle i.e. 'the locus of a point which is equidistant from a fixed point' in his own language. He will probably describe it by the type of ride it gives i.e. a 'not bumpy ride' (see Fig 4.5).

Fig 4.5

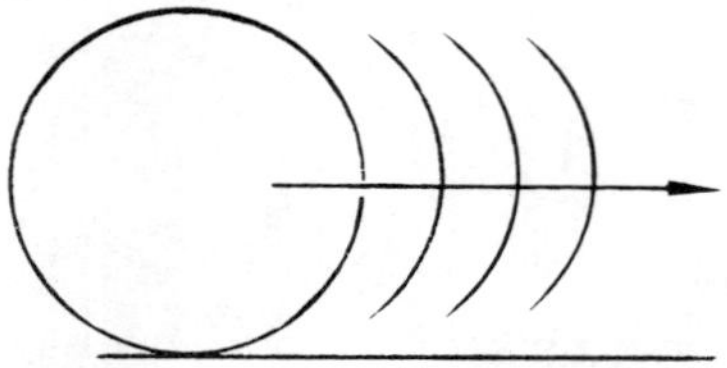

So, as the child builds or makes models, he is intuitively sorting shapes for their various properties and can be encouraged to verbalize these. He will also sort these shapes according to what they do i.e. roll or slide. Here the teacher can encourage the child to make a collection of shapes that roll and to talk about the different ways in which they roll i.e. the cylinder rolls in a straight line but the cone rolls round in a circle. He will find that some shapes, the sphere, ellipsoid and ovoid, have no flat surfaces at all and, again, roll in different ways. He will probably call the sphere a 'ball shape' to begin with and the ovoid an 'egg shape'. If possible he should have experience of playing with a rugger ball, the ellipsoid, and seeing how differently it rolls and bounces from the sphere.

Shape toys and equipment

One shape toy that should be in every nursery school is the posting box. There is a very good example of this toy on the market made from good quality wood with a collection of different lids and many shapes to 'post' through them (see Fig 4.6). Some of the lids have a very

Fig 4.6

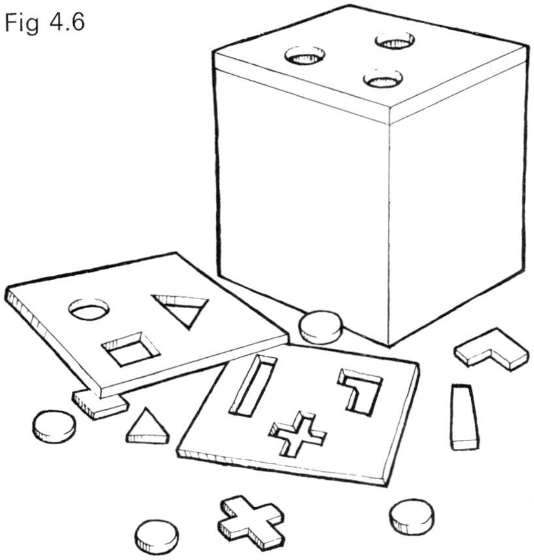

simple selection of holes in them, some have three holes that are all the same shape and others have more complicated shaped holes. The box can be used by very young children with one of the first type of lids and the teacher can observe if they recognize that the sphere will go through the circular hole and the triangular prism through the triangular hole etc. or whether they are still at the stage of trying to push any shape through any hole. The lids with three congruent holes can be used with slightly more advanced children to see if they recognize that the holes are the same and that they must therefore find three solids of the same shape. The more complicated lids can be used to test the child whose appreciation and understanding of shape is much further developed. The children can also be encouraged to produce shapes similar to these posting bricks out of playdough or plasticine or to see if they can find similar shapes in their box of building bricks or in the shapes-corner.

Some of the equipment used for sorting will also provide opportunities for work with shape e.g. the Attribute Blocks mentioned earlier which can be sorted into circular, triangular, square, rectangular and hexagonal prisms. These, and the ends of the building bricks, can be used to draw round i.e. to produce two-dimensional shapes.

Off-cuts of wood can be used in this way for 'printing' by dipping the wood into thick paint and then applying to paper as one does with a potato print. Using wooden shapes like this can result in shape-patterns and these can be the repetitive patterns mentioned earlier for work on ordering (see Fig 4.7). Wooden or plastic mosaics can also be

Fig 4.7

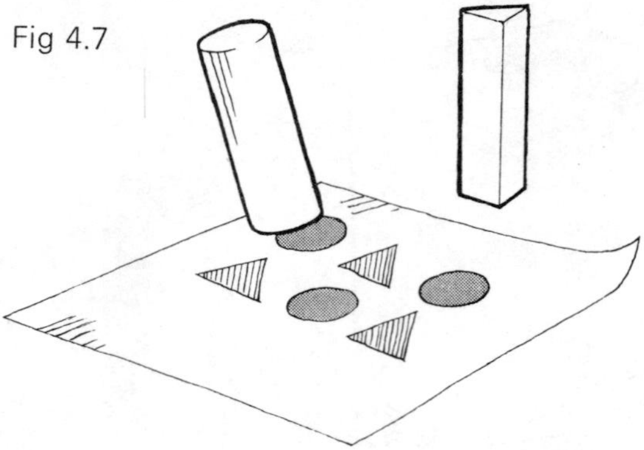

used for ordering patterns as well as for making regular and semi-regular tessellations. Children can be given a selection of brightly coloured sticky paper mosaics to make pictures with and can be encouraged to discuss the shapes that they have used for various parts

Fig 4.8

1 circle 5 rectangles 6 triangles

of the picture (see Fig 4.8). Again, they can be helped to find similar shapes in their everyday world e.g. rectangular doors, windows, tabletops; circular wheels, hoops, plates, drums, buttons; square table mats, floor tiles, box lids; triangular road signs, roof shapes, musical instruments, or to cut examples of familiar shapes out of magazines to make a *Book of Circular* (*or Rectangular, or Triangular*) *Shapes.*

The straightsided shapes can be made using wooden or plastic meccano-type struts. Making shapes in this way will emphasize the fact that they need three struts to make a triangle, four to make a quadrilateral etc. By watching children attempt to make rectangles the teacher will be able to see whether they have grasped the equality of opposite sides i.e. do they automatically choose equal pairs of struts or do they choose any lengths at first and have to be helped to choose equal ones. As they make shapes from these struts they can be helped to appreciate the rigidity of the triangle and that if they make a rectangle it will distort into a parallelogram unless they put in a diagonal i.e. cut it into two triangles (see Fig 4.9). It is, of course, the

Fig 4.9

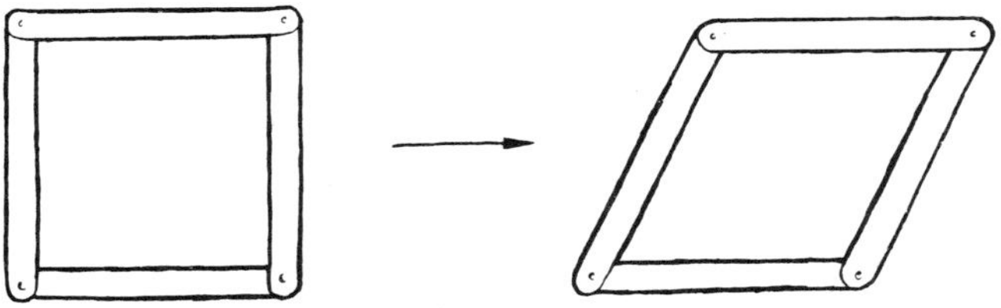

rigidity of the triangle and its resultant importance to building that has made this shape so vital to man and made it so interesting to the ancient Egyptians and Greeks who discovered many theorems connected with the triangle which many secondary children spend hours learning even now. If we look around us we can see many examples of the triangle used for rigidity e.g. the black beams in the walls of Elizabethan houses, in gates, bridges, the jib of a crane, electricity pylons etc. By choosing struts of different lengths the children can make different types of triangles. If they choose three equal lengths

Fig 4.10

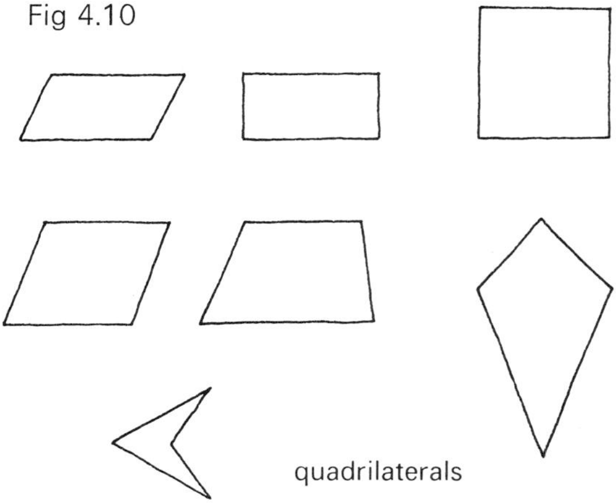

quadrilaterals

they will make an equilateral triangle, but if only two of their three struts are equal in length the resulting triangle will be an isosceles one. The word 'isosceles' is, of course, made from two Greek words meaning 'equal' and 'legs' and so an isosceles triangle is one with equal legs. The children can also be encouraged to make all the different types of quadrilaterals e.g. the parallelogram, rectangle, square, rhombus, trapezium, kite, arrowhead etc. (see Fig 4.10). They will incorporate many of these simple shapes into the models of lorries, aeroplanes, toy furniture etc. that they make with the struts and the teacher can talk about these models with them and see if they can recognize and name the shapes that they have used.

Shape in movement

Movement sessions will provide the teacher with more opportunities to use shape words and help the children to understand their meaning. They can be encouraged to join hands and form a large circle or, in smaller groups, to make a series of circles. Hoops can be used to remind them of the shape that they are trying to form and the personal involvement in physically making this shape will help them to understand its formation. Sometimes the teacher may ask the children to run round the outside of the circle or all to hop or dance round in a circle. Sometimes she may want them to group in fours and to stand at the corners of squares. They can be encouraged to roll themselves into tight balls like the sphere they were looking at earlier in the day or to be windmills with their arms making circles in the air like the windmill in the story they have just heard. Hoops can be bowled along and tyres used to wriggle through or jump into in outdoor play. There may be rectangular mats for individual children to sit on and bigger ones to put by some of the pieces of apparatus in use. The children may recognize the beanbags as being squares of material sewn together and the shapes of different types of bags may be discussed.

When children are painting or drawing they should be provided with a choice of different shaped pieces of paper so that sometimes they may choose to use a circular or triangular piece of paper rather than always using a rectangular one. The shape printing using the ends of solid shapes referred to earlier can also be done using open or hollow shapes such as the centres of toilet rolls. These can result in attractive designs consisting of different coloured circles (see Fig 4.11). Another painting activity which will help children with their understanding of shapes is finger painting. Here the children can be encouraged to dip their fingers in brightly coloured paints and then trace out on paper particular shapes just as later on in the infant school they will be encouraged to get the feel of the shape of their numerals and letters by tracing out these shapes with wet or paint covered fingers.

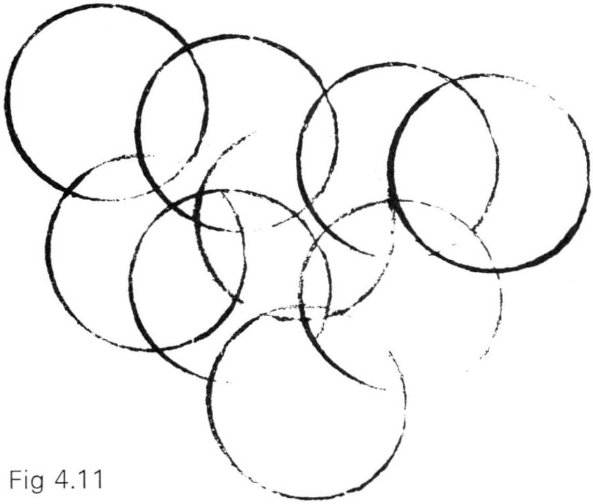

Fig 4.11

Sometimes they can be directed to make pictures or patterns using straight lines only and sometimes using only curved lines. Most attractive designs can be made by dropping handfuls of paper drinking straws onto well glued coloured paper backgrounds. Collages made from odds and ends of dress materials or from seeds and pulses or junk materials such as paperclips and buttons will also provide opportunities to discuss and compare shapes.

Symmetry

Many of the shapes that the children see about them, many of the ones that they will make or draw and many of their patterns possess a rather special property: they are symmetrical i.e. they all possess some type of balance. In order to assist young children in their appreciation of symmetry the nursery teacher herself needs to understand the different types of symmetry and to realise why symmetry is an important part of mathematics. So much work on symmetry tends to be encouraged with young children with no real appreciation of its development and progression. The simplest type is bilateral symmetry (see Fig 4.12). As its name suggests, it is two-sided symmetry i.e. the two halves of a shape or picture balance each other completely. This is sometimes referred to as line symmetry since there is a line or axis that cuts the shape into two identical halves. It is also called mirror symmetry, because if a mirror were placed on the axis of symmetry, the reflection would complete the shape. The other name for this very simple type of balance is symmetry of left and right which tends to imply that the axis of symmetry will always be vertical. This is not so; the axis can be horizontal or in any direction, it is the balance that is important. Very many objects in the child's everyday life will display

Fig 4.12

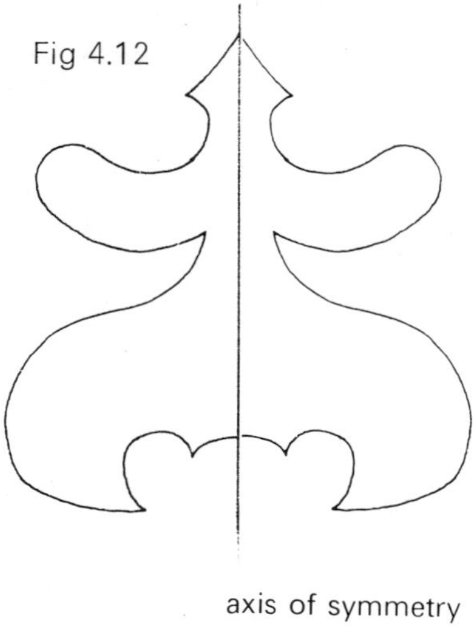

this type of symmetry and many of his own drawings and paintings will also be symmetrical. If we think of the child's home, the building itself may be one of a pair of semi-detached houses i.e. it is a mirror image of its partner. Within the house the beds, chairs, tables, bookcases, sideboards, lampshades, cups and saucers, cooking

Fig 4.13

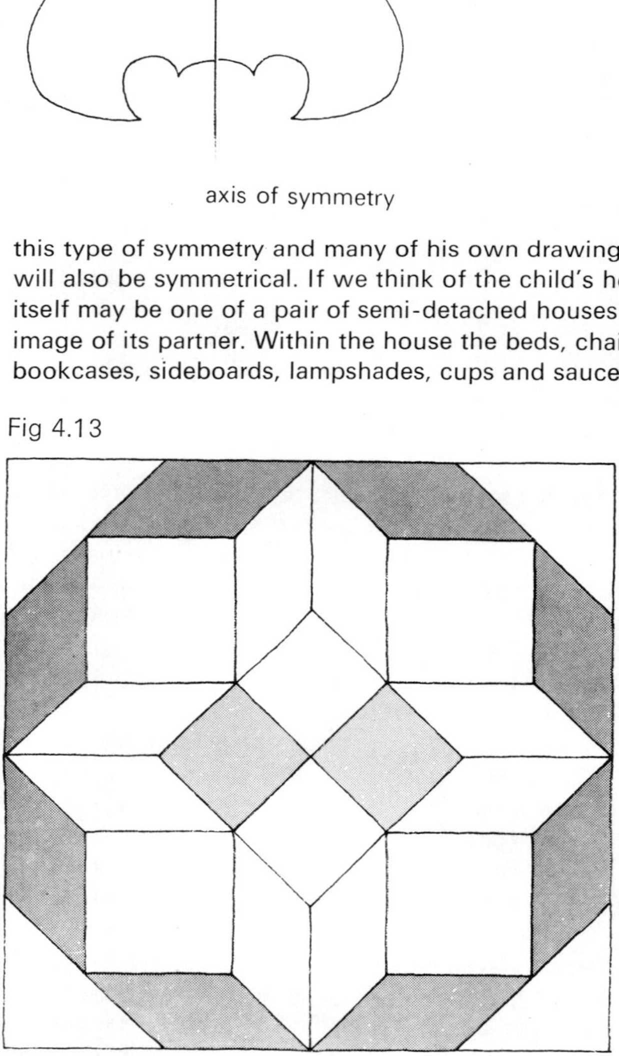

utensils etc. will be symmetrical, three-dimensional shapes which are balanced about a central plane. Many of the things he sees on his way to school will also be symmetrical and even his own body is almost symmetrical. In the same way most of the furniture and contents of the nursery classroom will also have this type of balance. Again, by discussion, the teacher can help the child to appreciate this balance in the world about him and help him to reproduce it for himself (see Fig 4.13). As the child plays with floor or table mosaics and forms shape patterns these will often be symmetrical and by applying blots of paint to paper and folding the paper while the paint is still wet he can produce fascinating paint-devils sometimes reminiscent of butterflies' wings (see Fig 4.14). Folding and cutting

Fig 4.14

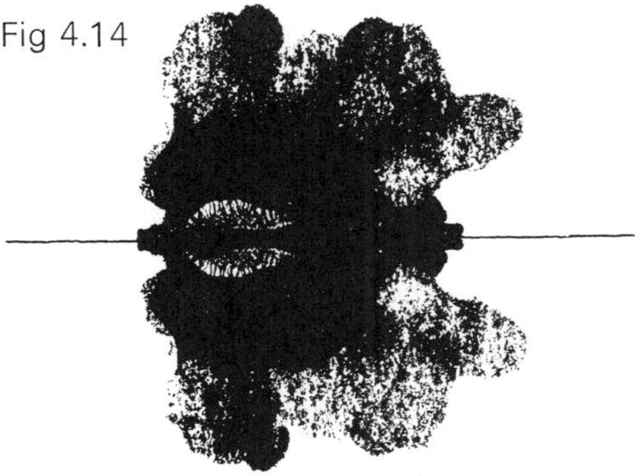

paper can also produce delightful symmetrical shapes and these can lead the child on to making highly decorative masks and decorations (see Fig 4.15).

Many of the shapes and patterns that the child will be familiar with will have more than one axis of symmetry. Nature provides us with many examples e.g. the iris head mentioned in an earlier chapter with its three axes of symmetry or the snow crystal with six. It should be noticed that if a shape has more than one axis of symmetry these all meet at one point which is called the centre of symmetry. Again, patterns will be made by the children which have two or more axes and, by folding paper more than once and cutting, attractive symmetrical shapes will be produced (see Fig 4.16).

There is another, more complicated, type of symmetry which young children may be able to appreciate but not verbalize. This is rotational symmetry, the sort of balance found in a letter Z, the Isle of Man symbol and many trademarks e.g. the woolmark and the sign of the National Westminster Bank (see Fig 4.17). Here the balance is about a point rather than about an axis. The shape can be rotated about that central point and will fit on to itself a certain number of times before it returns to its original position e.g. the letter Z will fit

Fig 4.15

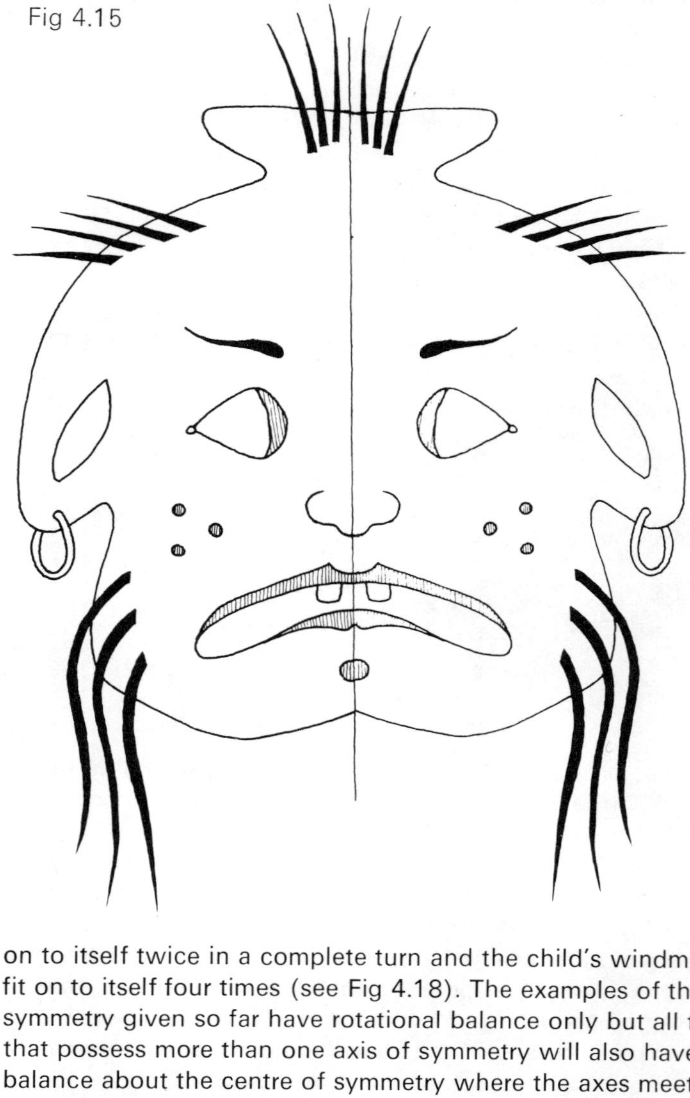

on to itself twice in a complete turn and the child's windmill toy wil· fit on to itself four times (see Fig 4.18). The examples of this type of symmetry given so far have rotational balance only but all the shapes that possess more than one axis of symmetry will also have rotational balance about the centre of symmetry where the axes meet. So some shapes have an axis of symmetry only e.g. the letter T. Some have rotational symmetry only e.g. the letter Z, but many have both types e.g. the iris head with its three axes and rotational symmetry of order three i.e. it fits on to itself three times in a complete turn. The shapes with rotational symmetry only cannot be produced by folding and cutting paper and will probably not be intuitively made by the child as patterns or paintings but he is quite likely to appreciate their balance and to recognize their particular type of symmetry especially if he can handle and rotate them himself.

Fig 4.16

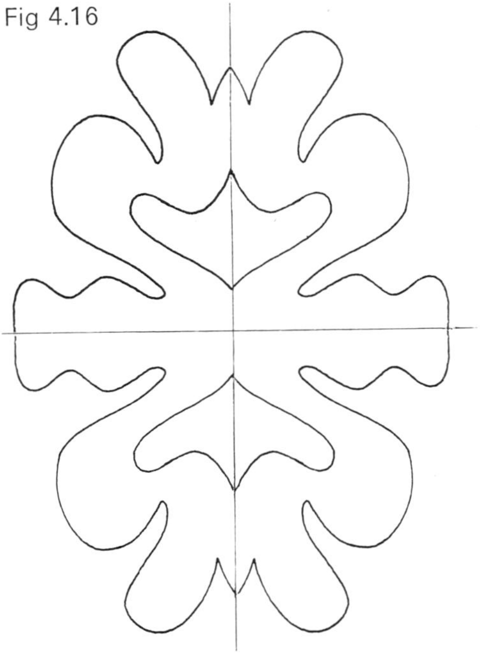

2 axes of symmetry

Fig 4.17

Fig 4.18

The older child can be encouraged to complete shapes with one or more axes of symmetry when given half or a quarter of the shape and to complete shapes with rotational symmetry drawn on squared paper, made on a nailboard with rubber bands or made out of gummed shapes (see Fig 4.19). In the infant and junior school, children will be

Fig 4.19

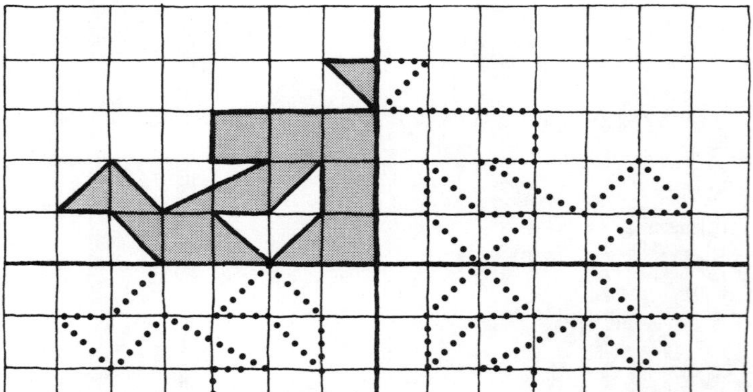

helped to recognize symmetrical letters and numerals and to make up symmetrical words and numbers e.g. NOON, BOB, 1691, 11 etc. (see Fig 4.20). All this work is fun and produces pleasing designs or results

symmetrical words and numbers

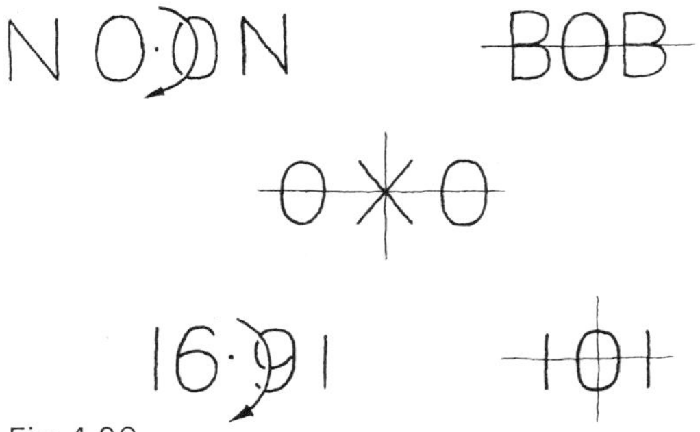

Fig 4.20

in interesting collections and charts but also has great importance in modern geometry. If we look at the symmetry of two simple geometrical shapes, the isosceles triangle and the parallelogram, this importance will become clear. The name of the isosceles triangle, as we have seen, tells us that it has equal legs, but if children of seven or eight years are given a variety of isosceles triangles, some acute angled and some obtuse angled, and asked to fold them on their axes of symmetry they will intuitively discover that these triangles probably have a lot more properties. As they fold the triangles they will see that:

i the base angles fit on to one another and so are probably equal

ii the axis of symmetry cuts the base into two equal pieces because these, again, fit on to one another

iii the axis cuts the base at right angles since these angles are equal but together make a straight line just as two right angles do when two cuboids are put side by side

iv the axis cuts the angle at the apex into two equal parts

v the axis cuts the whole triangle into two congruent triangles.

So all the properties of an isosceles triangle that most secondary children prove are true using the traditional formal proofs, can be intuitively discovered by a junior school child just by folding the triangle on its axis of symmetry. An equilateral triangle has three axes of symmetry and so many more facts can be discovered by folding three times (see Fig 4.21).

If we now look at a parallelogram that has no right angles and does not have all its sides equal i.e. one that is neither a rectangle nor a rhombus, we find we have a geometrical shape with no axes of symmetry, but just rotational symmetry. Many children, and many adults, feel that the parallelogram has axes and so it is essential for them to be able to handle one cut out of paper and to fold it on its diagonals, or lines parallel to its sides etc. in order to convince

Fig 4.21

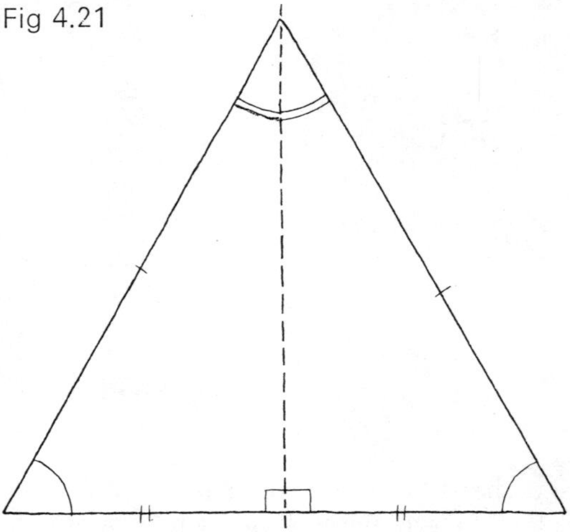

symmetry of the isosceles triangle

Fig 4.22

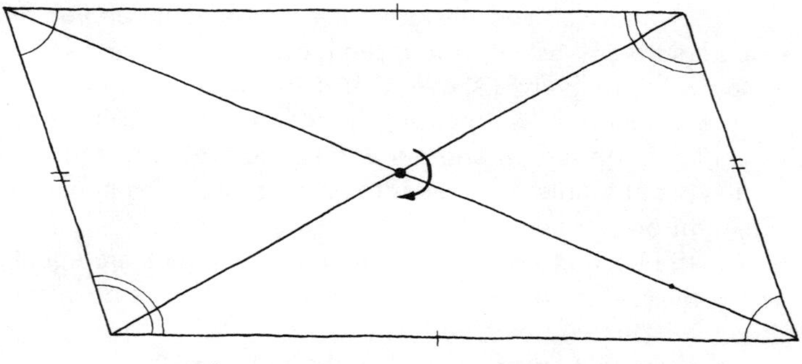

rotational symmetry of the parallelogram

Fig 4.23

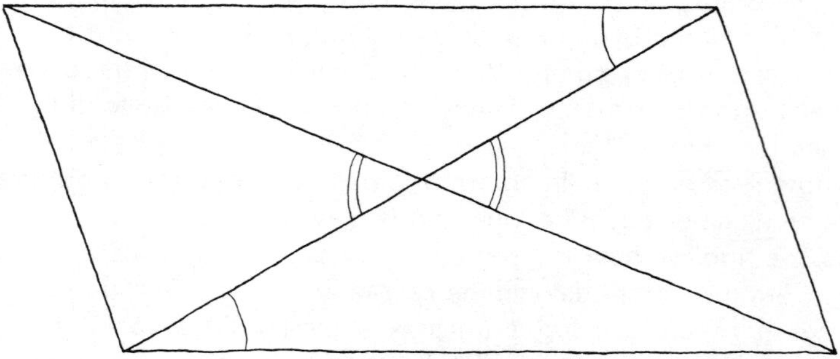

alternate angles and vertically opposite angles

themselves that, so long as it is not a rectangle or a rhombus, it has no axes of symmetry. To find its centre of rotational symmetry we must draw in the diagonals and find where these cross each other. The parallelogram can be pinned, through this centre, on to a sheet of paper and drawn round. Now it can be rotated about that centre and its properties intuitively discovered. As it rotates we see that its opposite sides fit on to one another and so are probably equal in length, its opposite angles are probably equal, its diagonals probably bisect each other, alternate angles are equal, vertically opposite angles are equal, and there are many congruent triangles (see Fig 4.22). This may be the first time that a junior child has met vertically opposite angles or alternate angles and from this he could be led to investigating whether these types of angles are always equal (see Fig 4.23). Again, all the properties of the parallelogram can be discovered by means of its symmetry. This type of geometry has become part of many 'modern' O-level syllabuses, leaving the more traditional formal proof for those children who are able to go further with their mathematics. So symmetry is a powerful geometrical tool, helping children to discover properties of shapes but, it must be stressed, not to prove that these properties hold for every such shape. Symmetry also has applications in further mathematics e.g. in curve sketching, and in integration, and in crystallography and the study of the structure of atoms and molecules.

Summary

Just as with number and measurement, we have seen that vital introductory work on shape can be attempted with pre-school children. By allowing them to handle shapes of all kinds, by providing large shapes for them to crawl through and to investigate from the inside as well as from the outside, by encouraging them to cut paper and to mould clay or plasticine and by helping them to discuss the properties of these shapes, we can help to lay a sure, practical, foundation for later, more formal work. This awareness of shapes will not only lead on to later geometry but will be of use to the child in his future life whether he becomes an architect, an engineer, a joiner, metal-worker, decorator, furniture manufacturer, machine operator or home-maker.

5

Recording and records

Children's recording

Nursery teachers often ask how much recording can be expected from pre-school children and some nursery teachers are very emphatic that recording is just not suitable for such young children. There are, however, some types of very simple recording that are possible and worthwhile in the nursery school. The actual set of blue things that the child has made or the actual tower that he has built are in themselves recordings and can be used as such. Other children can be invited to 'come and see what Tom has done' and encouraged to comment on it and, perhaps, to offer opinions as to whether he has found as many blue things as Mary did yesterday. Tom's set can be kept to compare with other children's sets later on in the day, or even tomorrow i.e. 'Let's see if Dick has found more red things than Tom found blue things.' When keeping achievements such as these they should be labelled with the child's name. Even though most of the children in the class cannot read, their names should be used to identify their work so that they begin to recognize the shapes and patterns made by different names. If a child has made a very tall building or a very long train this can be kept for the rest of the day and used as a measure to compare with other things in the room. The children can discover that it is taller than Susan but not quite as tall as John or that the train is longer than Harry's scarf. Some children may set to work to see if they can build taller towers or longer trains. This type of recording is temporary only but well worth using.

Pictorial recording

Often when the children make sets of, say, red things or things that roll, the teacher will encourage some of them to make a pictorial recording of what has been done. This is good at this stage provided she does not expect the child to be able to produce a drawing of the correct number of objects. To do this the child needs to be able to make a one–one correspondence and if there are more than six or seven objects in the set he may not be able to do this. If there are a small number, say three or four, he may be able to recognize that number and reproduce it. So the teacher must be prepared to accept a set of correct coloured shapes as a recording without necessarily having the correct number in the set. Sometimes she can point out that there is one more in the set than the child has drawn and with some children whose span of concentration is long enough she can help them to actually match the objects by putting them against the drawings and they can see that there are more. Even then, when they have seen that they should really draw more, they may lose interest and walk away before it is done. They have made their attempt at recording and at that stage that is enough. Later, in the infant school, we can expect more.

Set graphs and block graphs
These sets and drawings are the very beginning of 'Pictorial Representation' i.e. the very beginning of graphs. These graphs are pictures of relationships between the members of two sets and, as we have stressed before, mathematics is concerned with relationships. The related sets could be the set of children in a particular group and the set of their birthday months. The relationship between these two sets could then be 'was born in'. This could be recorded in the very simplest type of graph i.e. a set graph. It could arise from a particular child's birthday and discussion among the children as to when their birthdays are. The teacher needs to keep a careful check on this type of discussion to help children who do not really know when their birthday is and to make sure no one, in their enthusiasm, claims more than one birthday in the year! After this preliminary talk, encouraging individual children to express themselves in words and encouraging the others to listen to what they have to say, the children can be asked to stand in sets, i.e. those whose birthdays are in March to stand by the wendy house, those who were born in April by the water trough etc. By doing this the children have formed a physical set graph but, so that they can stand back and see the graph, each child can be given some token to put inside a hoop or loop of brightly coloured string that represents their birthday month. The hoops can be pulled closer to each other and the complete graph seen (see Fig 5.1). The tokens used could be the children's names written on cards or, perhaps, the picture labels that are used to indentify their coat-pegs in the cloakroom. In this way, each child can find his token and where he stood in the original set graph. The children can now discuss which month they think has the most birthdays, which the fewest etc. This will be good pre-number experience and may lead to a matching exercise i.e. putting the tokens side by side to make sure whether there are more birthdays in May or in June. If this matching is done with all the months the result is another simple kind of graph; the beginnings of a block graph (see Fig 5.2). As mentioned in Chapter 2,

Fig 5.1

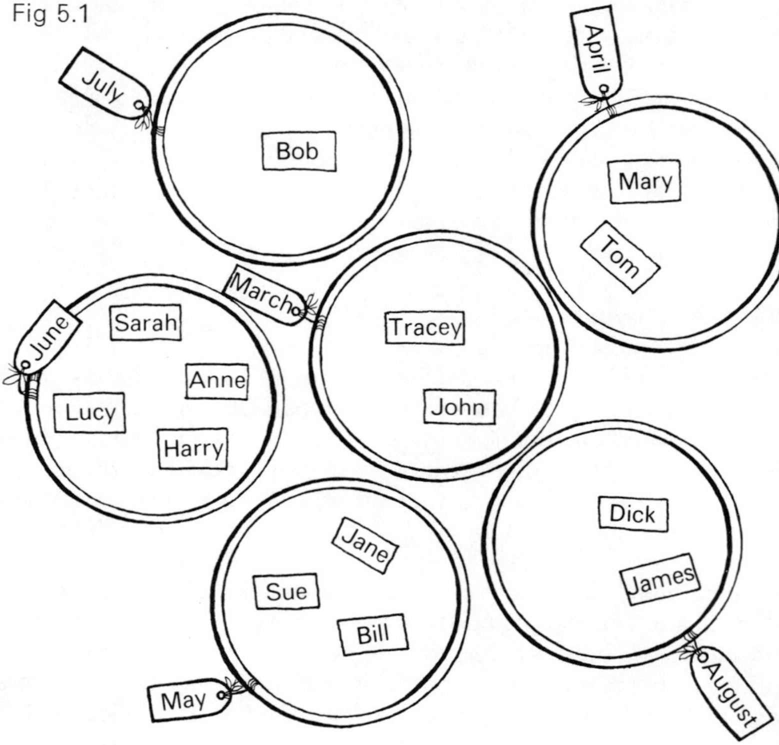

Fig 5.2

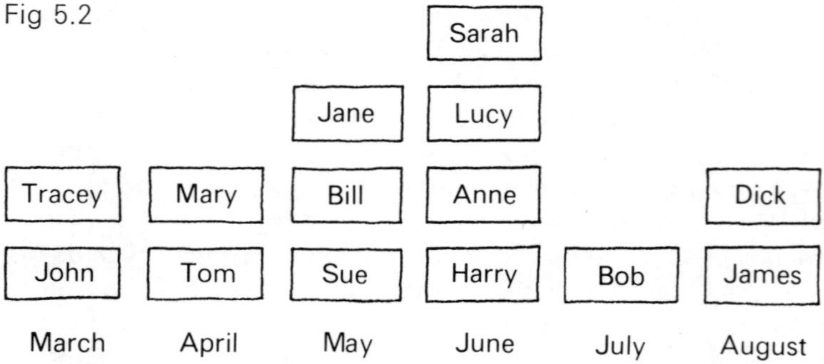

these graphs give us opportunities to 'find the difference' i.e. one aspect of subtraction. Two columns of tokens side by side will show the matched ones and the unmatched few which are 'the difference'. The graph can also be used for ordering practice i.e. putting the columns of tokens in order of height.

In the infant school, after the graph has been made, it will be used for discussion and computational practice i.e. 'how many birthdays in May and June together?' and the children will be encouraged to write a 'white paper' describing how the graph was made and what they discovered from it. The children will also be encouraged to display the information in more than one way so that the two types of graphs can be compared and discussed as to which shows the information more clearly. With pre-school children there will be a certain amount of discussion about the recording and the 'white paper' will be verbal, not written. We would certainly not expect a further graph to be made and compared at this stage. Flannelgraphs or magnetic boards are useful for this type of simple recording as they can be quickly brought into use as the teacher sees the opportunity to capitalize on the children's interests.

Matching graphs

Another very simple graph that can be used as a recording in the nursery school is a matching graph (see Fig 5.3). Here the children

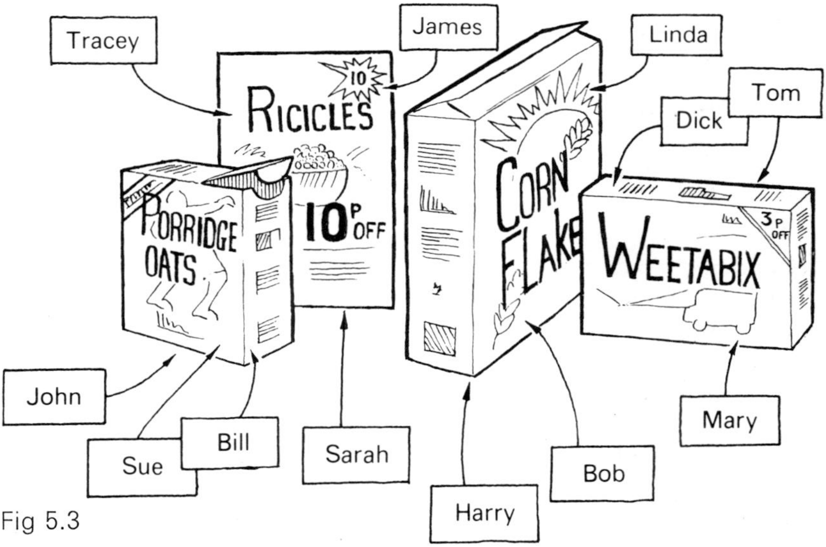

Fig 5.3

match themselves or their symbol to their particular choice. If the chance to use this has arisen from a discussion on favourite breakfast cereals, the teacher will put out on a table, or on the floor, empty cereal packets and the children will match themselves to their choice using lengths of coloured wool or tape which they will attach to the carton with Blutack. Again, so that they can all have a full view of the complete graph, they can replace themselves by their name card so that they can walk round the table or sit on the floor round the cartons and talk about what they have done. In the infant school this type of matching graph will be more organized so that the information can be more easily discovered. In the pre-school discussion of the graph the children will use such phrases as 'a lot of', 'not many', 'none at all' but in the infant school there will be actual counting, adding etc.

Partitioning graphs

In the chapter on pre-school activities the method of sorting within a set, i.e. partitioning, was mentioned. This can again be used to produce a partitioning graph. When the children are involved in pre-measurement sorting they may partition a set of building bricks into 'those longer than this one', 'those about the same length as this one', and 'those shorter than this one' (see Fig 5.4). This can be done on a

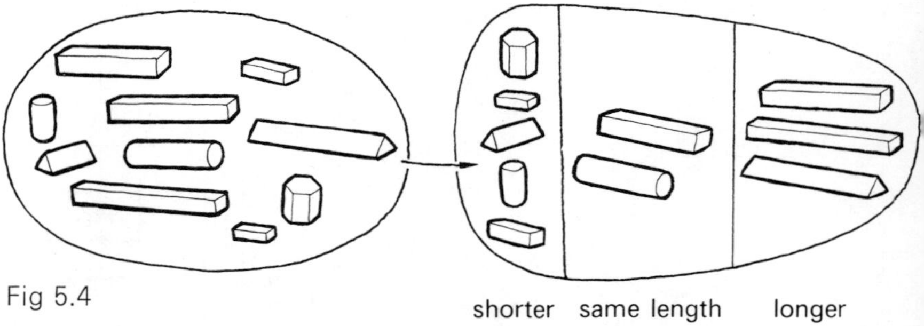

Fig 5.4

cupboard top and left as a recording to be added to during the day. This type of graph is often produced when children are packing bricks away, especially when they are putting the bricks into boxes with special sections for particular lengths e.g. the cuisenaire box. In all these graphs if the number of objects in a partition, or the number of matching threads to a certain packet, or the number of objects in a set is small enough to be recognized, this cardinal number should be used and the children helped to count the members of the set. Again, graphs like these can be used to give the children experience of the empty set, i.e. what we mean by nothing, by introducing a choice that no one will want.

Three-dimensional representations

A three-dimensional representation of the simple block graph can be made with the children by using a coloured cube to represent each child instead of his name card and the cubes can be built up in towers. This is best done using some type of cubes that slot into one another and so do not topple down when jogged by over enthusiastic participants (see Fig 5.5). Coloured beads can be threaded on to plastic

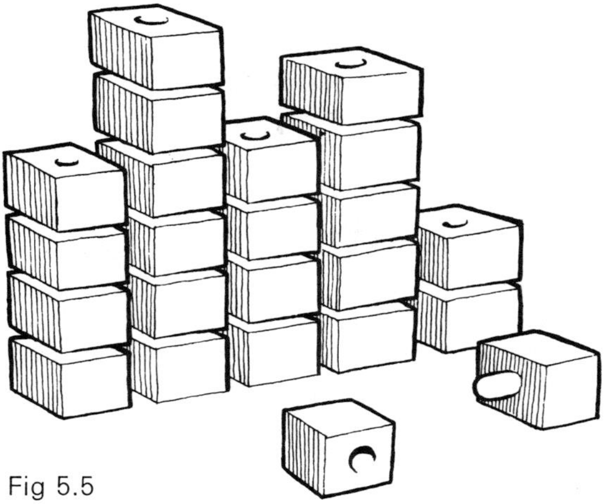

Fig 5.5

laces, pegs can be put into pegboard or washers placed on nailboards to represent the children, but this is a more abstract type of graph than the others as it will not be immediately apparent to the children which cube, bead etc. represents which child (see Fig 5.6). These graphs

Fig 5.6

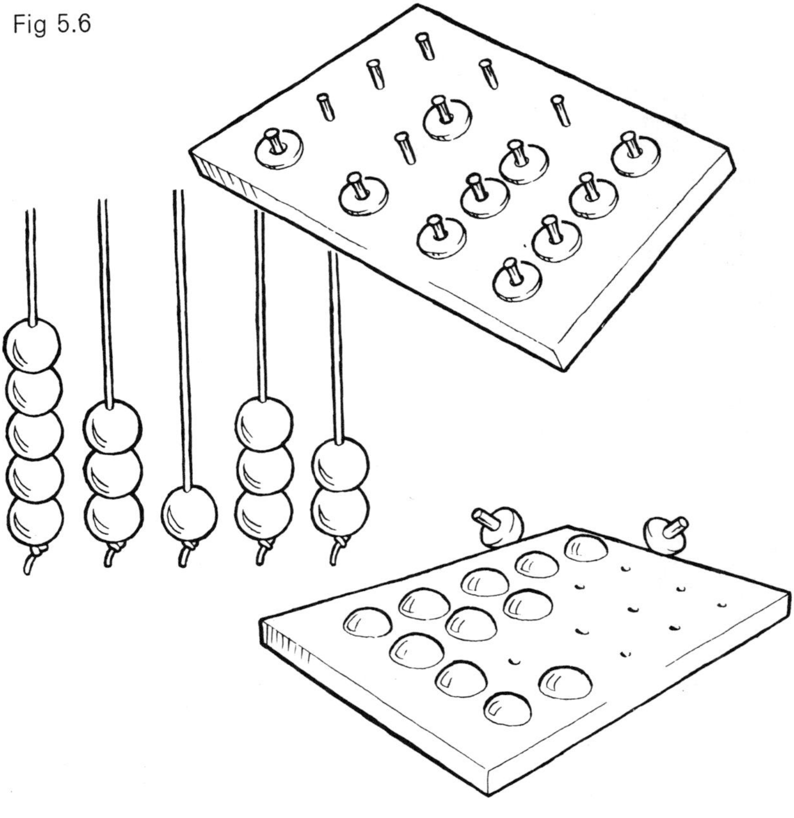

will, therefore, be more suitable for the children who can cope with this more abstract representation.

All children's drawings and paintings are also recordings; recordings that can be put on display or taken home to show the rest of the family. They can be recordings of the child's imagination or directed recordings e.g. a picture of his family which has been requested by the teacher after, perhaps, a discussion about who is the tallest and shortest in the children's families. Here the teacher may expect the child to draw his family in order of size but at this young age she is more likely to get a picture of his family in the order in which he thinks of them! These pictures will also record his perceptions, show how egocentric they are and how his awareness of the connections between things are developing e.g. his drawings of his family may show no ears, or the hair above the heads rather than a part of the heads. Some of these pictures will be worth keeping as records of the child's development.

Records worth keeping and handing on

If the child's experiences and development are worthwhile in the nursery school it seems a pity that some record of these should not be handed on to the infant school. So often the children who have had nursery experience are treated almost as nuisances by infant teachers because they have already experienced informally many of the things the infant teacher wishes to introduce in a more formal way. The child's ability to settle into the school atmosphere, to make relationships with his peers, to cope with his own buttons and shoe laces, to eat his school dinner etc. is fully appreciated but often his experiences with pre-number work, pre-measurement activities, shape recognition etc. is almost resented. By handing on with the child very simple records of his stage of development the nursery teacher could be of great help to the infant teacher. These records will help her to see where the child with his extra experiences will slot into her class and her routine. Obviously, within these records will be references to the child's ability to express himself in words and to his dexterity and manipulative skills but within this book we will examine mathematical records only, although many of these will have bearing on other areas also.

These records should not be merely the results of a checking up situation at the end of the nursery stage just before the child progresses into the infant school. They should be records of the teacher's observations of the child at play, of the child's verbal communication and of test situations which the teacher has introduced many times into the everyday activities as unobtrusively as possible. Should the teacher use only one or two checking up tests just before the child leaves the nursery stage she may choose times when the child is not feeling at his best or test materials which do not interest him or a time when he has his mind on some other project. Testing situations should only be used to confirm impresssions that the teacher has already gained through her observations over a long period.

What to record

What types of reactions and achievements are worth recording? If we consider pre-number work first and the various activities mentioned in Chapter 2, we would obviously want to record the child's ability to sort, to make a one–one correspondence, to put things in order, to count, to recognize the cardinal numbers of some sets, to appreciate the conservation of number and, perhaps, to appreciate the idea of inclusion. When a child sorts he is looking for relationships between things. At the nursery stage, when given a collection of objects such as buttons, coloured plastic shapes or shells, the child will not always begin to sort them but may begin to make patterns or pictures. The suggestion to sort may have to come from the teacher herself, and as stated in Chapter 2, the first type of sorting is finding more 'like this one', leaving the child to choose the relationship. This may be the relationship of colour, of material or size or use. So the first recording is whether a child appreciates these qualities of sameness e.g. does he recognize colour even though he may not know the name of that colour? By watching the child, the teacher will observe that he appears to recognize these attributes but she can only be sure after discussion with him. When he has carried out one classification such as this, can he re-sort the objects according to another property? This shifting from one criterion to another shows the mobility in the child's thought as well as the fact that he has noticed different properties of the objects. The classifications that the child appreciates will become more sophisticated as he becomes more aware of different attributes and so the type of classifications made can also be recorded. When he has made his set, does he recognize its cardinal number i.e. does he seem to recognize the two-ness of two etc? How many cardinal numbers can he recognize without counting? The nursery teacher must resist the temptation to set a standard for the children leaving her class i.e. she must not set a 'four-plus' or 'five-plus' test with its attendant 'passes' and 'failures'. Some of her children will easily recognize sets of five before they leave her while others will barely recognize sets of three but they will all have had experiences which will make them more ready for the formalization of sorting and number recognition in the infant school and it is this readiness that she is recording. She can watch and record the child's ability to make one–one correspondences from the many play situations where this arises and can test his appreciation of the conservation of number on many occasions. Often when a child is beginning to understand a concept such as this he may be able to use it in some situations but not be able to generalize it to all situations. The more opportunities he has of meeting the process of matching by one–one correspondence and the concept of the conservation of the number of members in a given set in everyday situations, the more easily he will learn to discover and use them. The concept of inclusion is a more difficult one and probably only a few of the nursery children will appreciate it. It was mentioned in Chapter 2 as a stretching activity for those children who seem to need some enrichment. It is the ability to recognize sets within sets e.g. the ability to recognize that whilst all cats are animals, not all animals are cats. Many opportunities will arise for the teacher to observe how the child copes with this. The toy farmyard or zoo animals provide good examples. Some children may not appreciate the differences between different types of animals but most will pen all the sheep together in one field and the cows in another. When it comes to tidying up, however, they will put the sheep and the cows together in the farmyard box. Again, it is only through discussion with the child, asking such questions as 'Is every cow a farmyard animal?', 'Is every farmyard animal a cow?' and 'Have you more cows or more farmyard animals?', that the teacher can really know whether the child has grasped this concept. Other opportunities for testing this may arise from tins of sweets containing chocolates and toffees, clothes in the dressing-up box that includes hats, shoes, dresses, trousers etc. a button box with different coloured buttons some having shafts and some holes, sets of cooking utensils in the wendy house with saucepans, frying pans and casseroles, the children themselves, some boys and some girls.

The child's ability to recognize the conservation or invariance of measures and shapes is also important. It was stressed in Chapter 3 that the measurement undertaken in the nursery school should be mainly concerned with comparisons and not with representations of measures by standard or abitrary units except for very simple representations such as spoonfuls, bucketfuls etc. used in very practical situations. The infant teacher will appreciate some indication in the child's nursery record of his understanding of the invariance of length i.e. can he recognize that two equal lengths remain equal in different positions?; of the invariance of mass, i.e. does he always understand that a mass of material remains the same whether it is in a large lump, a long snake or a collection of smaller pieces?; of the invariance of liquid or sand, i.e. does he realize that when liquid is carefully poured from a tall, narrow jug into a short, wide bowl, despite the difference in the level of the liquid, the quantity of liquid has not changed? (see Fig 5.7); of the conservation of area, i.e. has he made any progress towards appreciating that the pictures or patterns he makes out of the tangram pieces all cover the same area of table

Fig 5.7

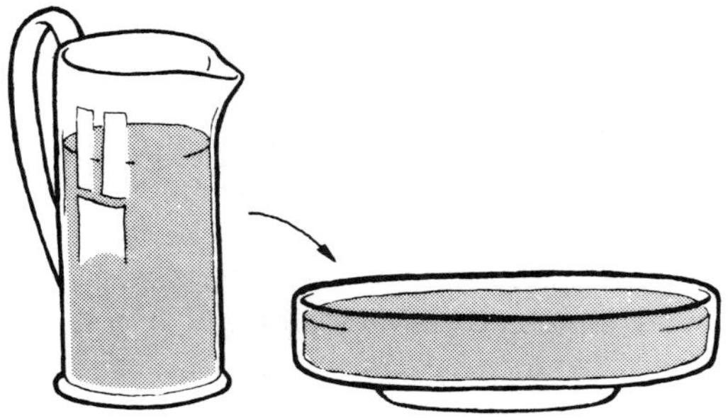

top or floor? These records will rarely be as simple as a tick to indicate that the child can understand these concepts. The nursery teacher will be more likely to record that the child appears to appreciate some of these in particular situations but not in others. This will indicate which situations the infant teacher can use as confidence builders and which she will need to help the child progress towards and with which he will need more experience. Some very helpful testing projects are suggested in the Nuffield Guides *Checking up I* and *Checking up II* but nursery teachers must remember that these tests were designed for primary school children and will need simplifying in materials and approach for pre-school children.

Appreciation of the constancy of shapes should develop during the nursery stage. The teacher can help the child to realize that the same article looks different when viewed from various angles by playing object recognition games with small groups of children. She can encourage children to describe a large wooden toy, paint container, cupboard, model etc. from their own viewpoints and to listen to other descriptions so that they appreciate that their friend sees a different view from theirs. They can move round the object and see that from some angles they can see its wheels but from others they cannot. Magazine pictures can be discussed and compared with similar articles in the school and, if possible, colour photographs of familiar articles can be used in conjunction with the articles themselves. Children can be asked to look at objects in the playground when they are on top of the climbing frame and then to view them from the swing and then from the playground seat. Various buildings can be discussed as they are seen from the classroom window and compared with how they look as the children pass them on their way to school. This will also involve perspective and the apparent difference in size of the same object viewed from different distances. Experiences of these apparent changes in looks and size can be built into the nursery programme and records kept of the children's comments and arguments used in discussions.

The child's ability to recognize simple three and two-dimensional shapes can also be recorded. When making patterns with plastic mosaic shapes he may be able to recognize which are triangles, squares or rectangles but can he carry this recognition over into the world about him, i.e. does he recognize the top of the road sign as a triangle? He may have difficulty in picking out building bricks with square end faces although he knows that the thermoplastic tiles on the floor are squares. Some children may still be at the stage of recognizing 'open' and 'closed' shapes or shapes with holes in them but not able to appreciate the difference between a circle and a square, while others may be able to recognize and name most shapes and describe some of their properties (see Fig 5.8).

Fig 5.8

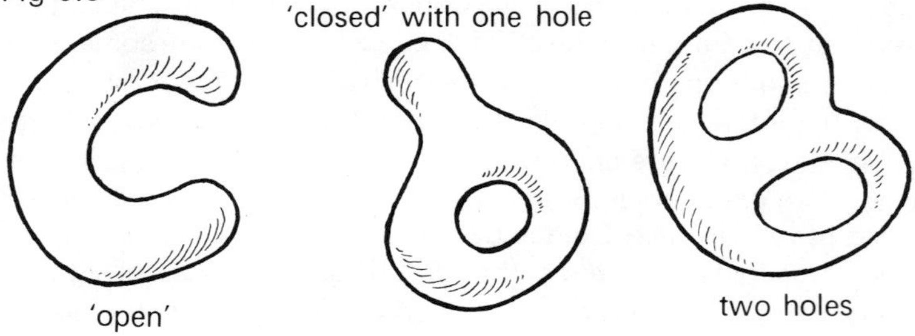

Records such as these will help the infant teacher build on the experiences of the nursery school. She will know that these children are ready to take on tasks that others cannot cope with yet and that she can expect them to understand language that children coming straight from home may not appreciate. By understanding and making allowances for their stage of development she can see that they are given work that is suitably challenging for them and can use their familiarity with certain situations and materials to encourage the other children to participate in activities and discussions. To build up the child's confidence in a new situation the teacher will encourage him to repeat some familiar experiences but by knowing his nursery school 'record' she will be able to avoid underestimating his ability. The daughter of a friend of mine came home from her first day at infant school very disappointed because she had not been able to cope with the simple number work expected of her. Her teacher, knowing that she had had pre-school number experience, set her the task of putting sticks in a series of numbered pots i.e. one stick in the pot marked '1', two in the pot marked '2' etc. to ten in the pot marked '10'. Susan had not been able to do this. Her mother was most surprised and asked her why she could not manage it. Susan's reply was 'Well, she only gave me forty-three sticks!' Susan's ability and understanding had been grossly underestimated.

6

Nursery incidents

In previous chapters we have looked at some of the mathematics that could be included in a nursery school programme. Some of it will arise naturally from the children's play, the teacher observing, supplying a suitable piece of equipment, asking a pertinent question or joining in the make-belief. At other times she will plan the introduction of mathematical experiences. Through the use of nursery equipment and happenings she will contrive discovery situations which will raise certain mathematical questions. Most situations, planned or arising naturally, will offer many mathematical opportunities and it is up to the individual teacher, knowing the development and attention span of her children, to decide whether to capitalize on some of these opportunities, just on one or on none at all. She must be sensitive to her children and their interests, judging when to interfere and when to observe from a distance so that she does not intrude on their make-belief and ruin their imaginative play. She should be aware of the mathematical potential in these situations but not be mathematically obsessed.

To complete this book on nursery mathematics we will look at a few nursery incidents and see what mathematical capital could be made from them.

Bath-time

Helen and Jane (both about four years old) decided that some of the dolls in the Home Corner needed a bath. They asked for warm water because it was a cold day and they did not want the dolls to catch a chill. The teacher pointed out that some of the dolls could not be washed safely and helped them to sort the washable ones, mostly plastic, from the non-washable ones like Teddy and Jemima, the rag doll. Helen fetched the wash-up bowl from the sink but Jane said that was not big enough and emptied the plastic baby-bath that had been used by another child as a bed for one of the bigger dolls. They decided to fetch the warm water in a bucket but found it was too heavy to carry when full. Jane suggested they should bring the baby-bath over to the bucket and tip the water into it but Helen pointed out that the baby-bath would then be too heavy to carry. They asked Mrs Howard, the nursery assistant, to carry it for them. She suggested they put on water-proof aprons and carried the bucket over to the Home Corner while they fetched them. Then she asked what they were going to use to wash the dolls with and Helen fetched some soap. Jane said the dolls' towels were not big enough to dry Mary-Lou, the biggest doll, and asked Mrs Howard for a bigger towel. She and Helen set about undressing the dolls. Helen had difficulty with Mary-Lou's jacket which had square buttons but Mrs Howard helped her with them. Jane began putting the dolls in the water all together but stopped because, 'They won't all go in'. Helen suggested two dolls at a time was enough but that Mary-Lou would have to be washed on her own. Jane used a flannel and Helen a sponge but they squabbled over the soap until Mrs Howard suggested they should fetch another piece from the cloakroom. When the dolls were washed and ready to be dressed again, the girls discovered that they had put all the dolls' clothes in a heap. This meant that the clothes had to be sorted and matched in size to the dolls. Jane soon lost interest so Mrs Howard suggested she made the dolls a nice hot drink after their bath. Jane put out some cups and pretended to pour hot milk from the saucepan into them. Mrs Howard helped Helen dress the other dolls and the two girls gave them their drinks.

There is a great deal of mathematical potential in this incident although far from all of it would be used with these children. The dolls were *sorted* and so were their clothes. There was some *matching* in that the girls fetched an apron each but Mrs Howard could have extended this by suggesting that they organized all the things they needed before they began bathing the dolls i.e. one apron each, one bar of soap each, one flannel or sponge each. Here too was a chance to comment on *equivalent sets*: two children, two aprons, two pieces of soap, two things to wash with (see Fig 6.1). With children whose span of concentration was greater, the clothes could also be matched with the dolls as they were re-dressed i.e. one pair of pants each, one dress etc. If Jane had not been tired she could have been helped to match the cups with the dolls when she made their drink and there could have been some discussion as to whether there were enough cups or too many. The dolls could have been *ordered* by size and this would have led to *comparisons of length* or height. There was some *simple measuring* in that Mary-Lou was seen to be the biggest doll, the size of the bath was discussed and the towels were too small. The bucket of water was *too heavy* for the girls to carry but Mrs Howard could have helped them to realize that if they put less water in the bucket it would have been lighter in weight and they could have carried it themselves and then gone back for more water. Jane did not seem to appreciate the *conservation of mass* when she suggested they

Fig 6.1

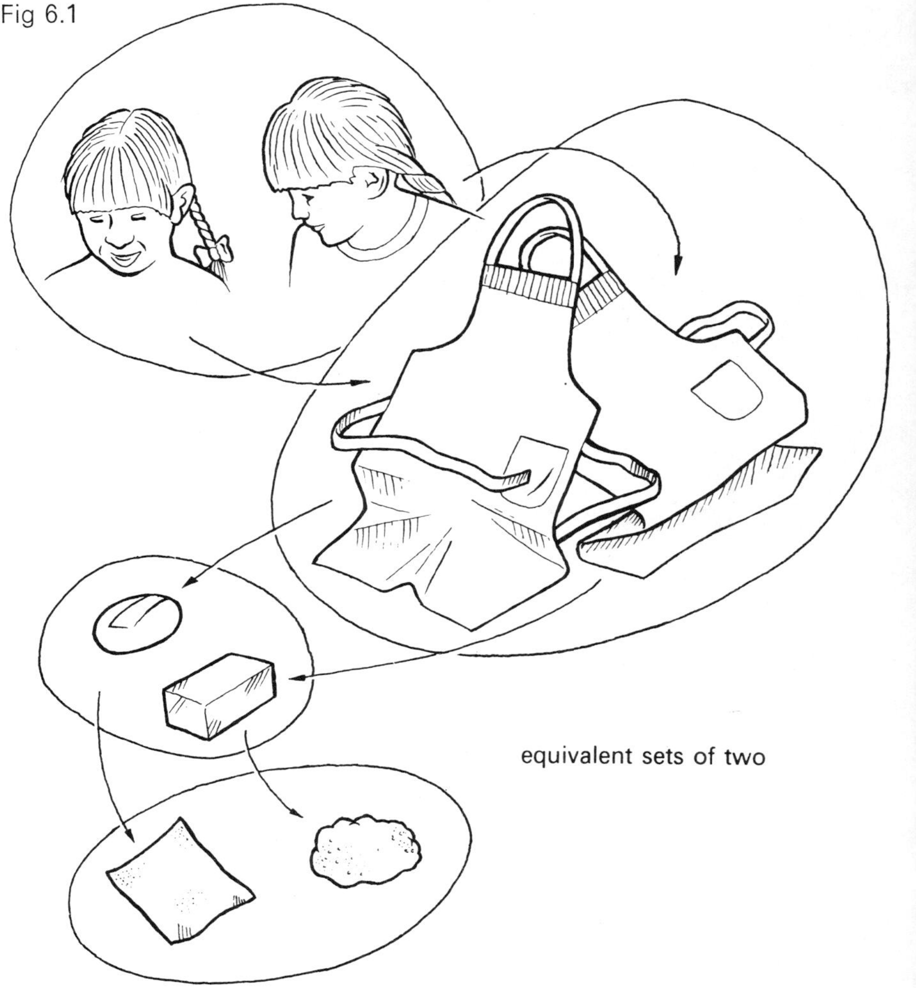

equivalent sets of two

might tip the water into the baby-bath but Helen did. They could have discussed how *hot* they wanted the water and been encouraged to test the *temperature* with their hands until it was right. There was some experience of *volume* in that Jane found that all the dolls would not fit into the bath together. The *shape* of Mary-Lou's buttons could have been commented on and why round ones were easier to cope with than square ones discussed. The washable and unwashable dolls could have been *counted* and the children helped to see that the washable dolls were *included* in the set of dolls (see Fig 6.2).

Playing with mosaics

Paul, who was three and a half, fetched the box of wooden mosaics

Fig 6.2

washable dolls included in the set of dolls

and tipped them out on the floor.

'This one's a roof-shape', he said as he turned over a big red, right-angled isosceles triangle.

'Can you find any more like that?' asked the teacher. Paul put out the big yellow, blue and green triangles beside the red one. Then he pushed them together and said, 'Look, they make a big square.' (see Fig 6.3).

'Are there any others that do that?' asked the teacher. Paul did not reply but collected all the square mosaics together and remarked that these were all smaller than the square he had made from the big triangles.

'How do you know they are all squares?' asked the teacher.

'Cos they are,' replied Paul. He then began fitting the squares together to make bigger squares and then put two rectangular mosaics side by side and said, 'These make squares, too.' Then he picked up two of the smaller triangles and was excited to see that they also made a square when put together. He looked at the original square he had made using the four big triangles and took two of the triangles, turned them round and fitted them together to make a square (see Fig 6.4).

'They all make squares,' he said.

'How many blue squares are there?' asked the teacher.

Fig 6.3

Fig 6.4

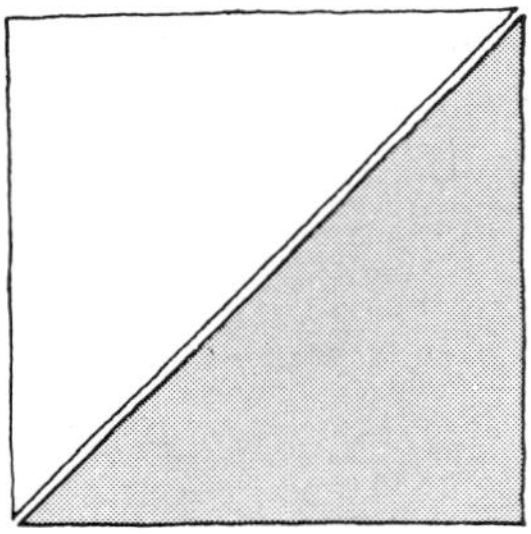

'Two,' said Paul, 'But I can make more if I put two blue roof-shapes together.'

Then he said 'I'm going to make a picture now,' and began picking out various shapes and colours, lost interest and wandered off.

(Paul's box of mosaics consisted of squares, rectangles and right angled isosceles triangles only. He would have been able to make pictures more easily if the set had included other shapes. His set was too limiting.)

Obviously this incident is full of *shape experiences* but other areas of mathematics could be brought in. Paul's description of the triangle as a 'roof-shape' was a good one which the teacher should have accepted and then introduced the correct name *triangle* as she talked with him. He was able to recognize *congruent* shapes but did not seem to recognize *similar* ones at first, although towards the end of the incident he was intuitively doing so. He could not give reasons for recognizing *squares* but this recognition was very secure and he was quite sure that the *rectangles* were not squares. He did not use the word rectangle and perhaps the teacher could have introduced it to see if he knew it. There was some *sorting* in this incident, mainly according to shape. Notice that the *classification of shape* was chosen by Paul. When the teacher asked him to find some more like his big red triangle he could have selected red shapes. Later on, the teacher did ask him to sort out the blue squares and he did this very successfully. He was gaining simple experience of *tessellations* as he fitted his shapes together and was also *comparing the size* of the squares. He showed his ability to recognize *sets of two* and could have been encouraged to *count* further. Although he could not make a picture from this limited set of mosaics he might have been able to make *simple row patterns* which would have led to the *ordering* of shapes to repeat the pattern. He might also have been able to point out other squares, rectangles and triangles in the room showing that his recognition of these shapes was not only as mosaics.

Building

John, Peter and Bobbie (all aged between three and four and a half)

Fig 6.5

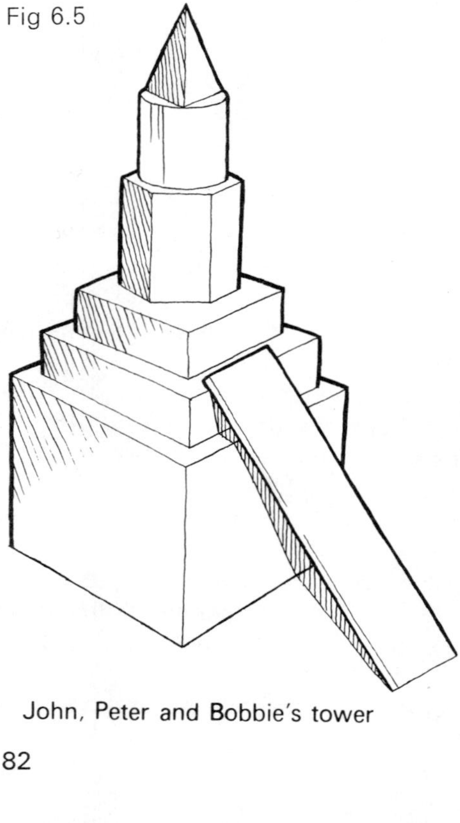

John, Peter and Bobbie's tower

were playing with the large building blocks. Between them they decided to build a tower. They chose a large cube for the base, then two cuboids, a hexagonal prism, a cylinder and finally a pyramid (see Fig 6.5). Peter, the eldest, fetched a long flat piece of wood and rested it against the tower so that it formed a ramp and suggested they ran the toy cars down this to see which was the fastest. They had great fun with this until Peter got too enthusiastic and knocked the tower down. The other two were very cross and although Peter said he would build it again, Bobbie walked off declaring that he was not going to play with Peter any more. Peter and John then built a new tower but left out the cylinder which had rolled away. Bobbie walked past a little later and remarked that the new tower was not so high as 'his' tower had been.

Again, this incident could be used as a springboard for *shape* work. First the *names of the shapes* used, getting the children to name them, or describe them, the teacher supplying the correct names if the children did not know them. The *reasons for choosing* these shapes could be discussed i.e. why begin with the large cube, and why finish with the pyramid? The teacher could have helped the children to see that they were putting flat *surfaces* on to flat surfaces and that the cylinder could not have been used on its side because that was a *curved surface*. No one noticed the cylinder *roll* away when the tower was knocked down or that it was the only shape that would roll. The *shapes of the faces* could have been identified and the fact that the tower stood *upright* linked with the *right angles* of the cuboids, Bobbie introduced *measurement by comparison* by saying he thought the second tower was not so high as 'his' had been. The tower could have been used to compare heights with other things in the room using '*taller than*', '*shorter than*' and '*about the same height as*'. The bricks used in its construction could have been compared for *height* and *length*. An adult could have helped the children realize that in building the tower they had *ordered* the bricks as the base of each one covered *less area* than the one below. The bricks could have been *counted* and others *added* to make it taller. The loss of the cylinder was a practical example of the 'take-away' aspect of *subtraction*. The *slope* of the ramp could have been altered by resting it on a *lower* brick or a *higher* brick. The *speeds* of the cars could not really be compared but the children were getting the impressions of speed from watching them.

Shoes (teacher planned)

Mrs White had been talking with a small group of children about their shoes. She was really rather tired of helping so many of them with their laces and buckles and was secretly wishing that more mothers would buy slip-on shoes for their children. Within this small group of children, two had lace-up shoes, two slip-ons and one had sandals with buckles. As the other children came in from the hall they noticed what sort of shoes they were wearing and Mrs White decided to make a *simple graph* of this with the children and to use this for some *early number work.* There were fifteen children in her section of the room. First she called them all together and asked them to look at each other's shoes and tell her if they were the same or different. Some of the children noticed the colours of the shoes but the ones in the original small group pointed out that it was how the shoes did up that mattered. Using the original five children as leaders, Mrs White then collected the children together in three *sets*, those with laces those with buckles and those with slip-on shoes. Susie was left on her own as she had a button on each of her shoes so she made a very special set. Mrs White then asked the children to stand in rows behind the leaders. The row of children with buckles was the longest but they were not sure if there were more with laces or more slip-ons. The teacher then suggested they all took off their shoes and left them in the rows (see Fig 6.6). Now they could all see the graph made from the shoes and they could *match across the rows* and see if there were more with laces or not. They found that there were *the same number* of pairs of

Fig 6.6

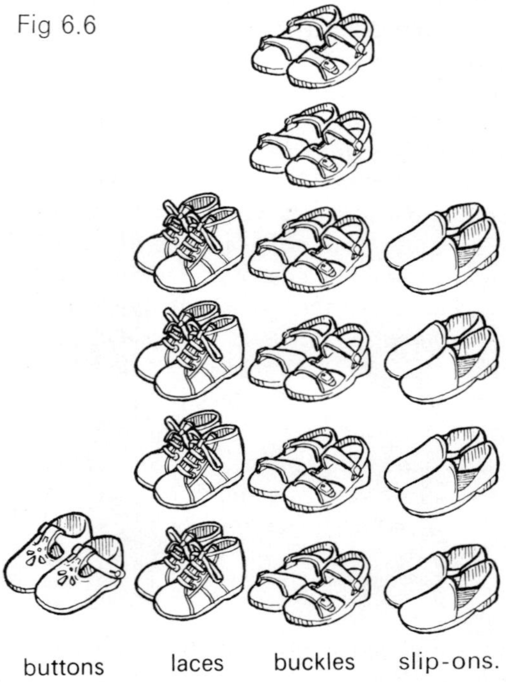

the shoe graph

shoes with laces as there were slip-ons. Some of the children said there were *four pairs* with laces and so Mrs White helped them *count* the pairs. The younger ones began to get bored so Mrs White asked each child to fetch two cubes from the storage box. They put the cubes where their shoes were and put their shoes on again. Mrs White had to help some of them with their laces and buckles and began to wonder if it had all been worthwhile! She called the six eldest children to her and let the others go off to play or paint. These six helped tidy the graph which now consisted of pairs of bricks and they spent a little more time on *counting* and comparing. They found there were *two more pairs* with buckles than pairs with laces and *three more pairs* with laces than buttons. James then put the columns *in order,* beginning with the *longest column*. Susie said there were two shoes in her column so they talked about pairs of shoes meaning two shoes but only one person. James and Peter said they would draw the graph so that it could be put on the wall. They decided it would be easier to draw squares for the cubes than draw the actual shoes. Peter did not draw enough shoes with buckles at first and Mrs White had to help him match the pairs of cubes to his pairs of squares before he accepted that he must draw another pair. Mrs White wrote the names of the children across their pairs of squares and drew symbols to represent the different types of shoes under each column. They pinned the graph upon the wall and Mrs White used it to do some counting with another group the next day. Hazel who had not been at school on the first day was in this group so they *added* her pair of shoes to the graph. This made the column representing the shoes with laces longer than the one representing slip-ons. While this group were talking about their shoes they noticed that Mary's shoes were *bigger than* Hazel's. Mrs White asked what they meant by bigger and they agreed that here they really meant *longer*. This led on to more work on comparisons of length.

Glossary

addend one of a set of numbers to be added e.g. $2+3=5$; 2 and 3 are addends.

addition an operation associated with the union of disjoint sets.

area measurement of surface covered.

associative property of addition the way in which any two out of three addends are associated does not alter their sum e.g. $(2+3)+4=2+(3+4)=(2+4)+3$.

associative property of multiplication the way in which any two out of three factors are associated does not alter their product e.g. $(2\times3)\times4=2\times(3\times4)=(2\times4)\times3$.

capacity measurement of space a container will hold.

cardinal number the number of a set, answering the question 'How many?'

circle set of coplanar points all at the same distance from a given centre point.

commutative property of addition the order in which two numbers are added does not alter their sum e.g. $2+3=3+2$.

commutative property of multiplication the order in which two numbers are multiplied does not alter their product e.g. $2\times3=3\times2$.

cone the solid formed by revolving a right-angled triangle about one of the sides containing the right angle.

congruent equal in all respects.

conservation the property of remaining unchanged in different circumstances e.g. the length of a pencil remains the same when that pencil is moved from one position to another.

coplanar all lying in the same plane e.g. all on the same table top.

cube a prism with six congruent square faces.

cuboid a prism with six rectangular faces which are congruent in opposite pairs.

cylinder a prism with circular end faces.

difference the cardinal number of the unmatched set when one set is compared with another set e.g. Fig a.

digit any one of the ten symbols 0, 1, 2, 3, 4, 5, 6, 7, 8, 9.

disjoint sets sets with no common members, e.g. Fig b.

Fig a

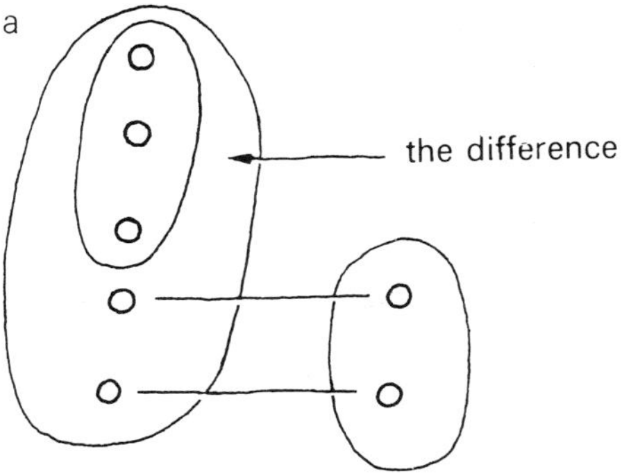

Fig b

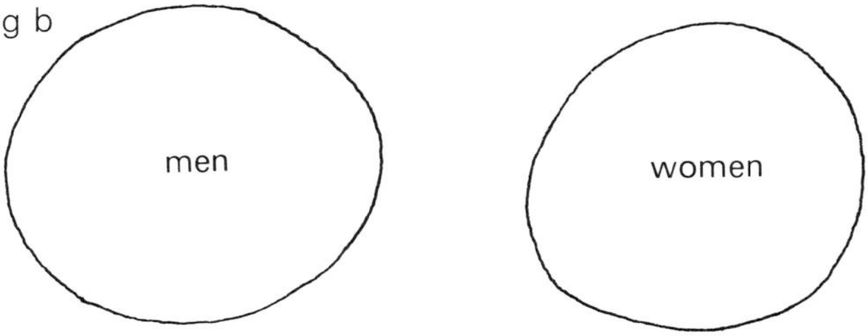

empty set set with no members e.g. children over 12 metres tall.
equivalent sets sets with the same cardinal number.
hexagon a six-sided plane shape.
matching putting each member of one set into correspondence with at least one member of another set e.g. Fig c.

Fig c

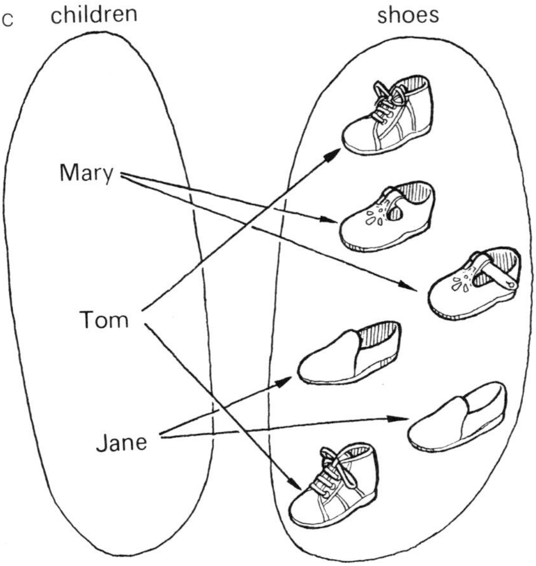

multiplication addition of equivalent sets.

one–one correspondence to each member of one set there is one, and only one, matching member of another set, e.g. Fig d.

Fig d

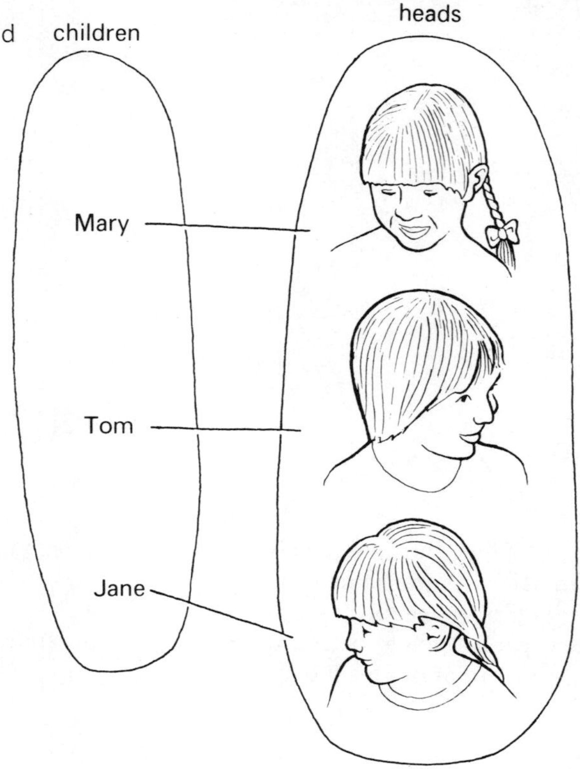

parallelogram a quadrilateral plane shape with opposite pairs of sides parallel.

partitioning separating a set into two or more disjoint subsets.

plane shape a two-dimensional shape.

prism a solid whose end faces are congruent and parallel and whose cross sections parallel to these end faces are also congruent to them.

pyramid a flat based solid with sloping sides meeting at an apex.

quadrilateral a four-sided plane shape.

rectangle a parallelogram whose angles are right angles.

relation a linking of the members of one set with those of another, e.g. Fig e.

rhombus a parallelogram with equal sides.

seriation ordering.

set a collection of distinguishable objects which may be concrete or conceptual.

Fig e

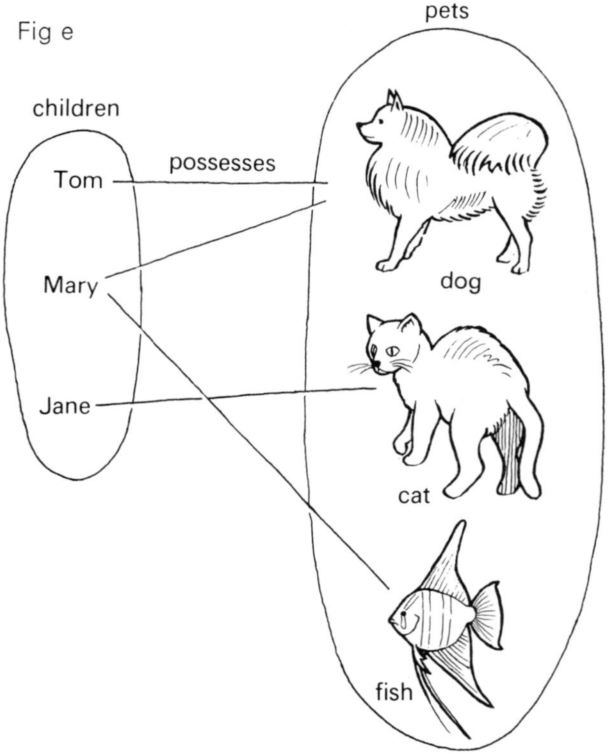

solid shape a three-dimensional shape.
sphere a solid formed by rotating a circle about a diameter.
square rectangle with equal sides.
subset a set of members contained within another set, e.g. Fig f.

Fig f

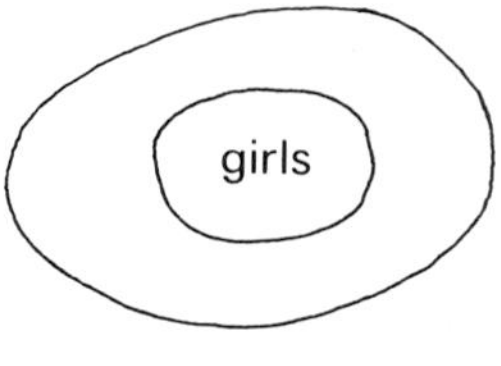

subtraction operation associated with the removal of a subset from a set, or with finding the difference between the number of elements in two sets, or with finding the cardinal number of the set that must be added to another to make it equivalent to a third set, see Fig g.

Fig g

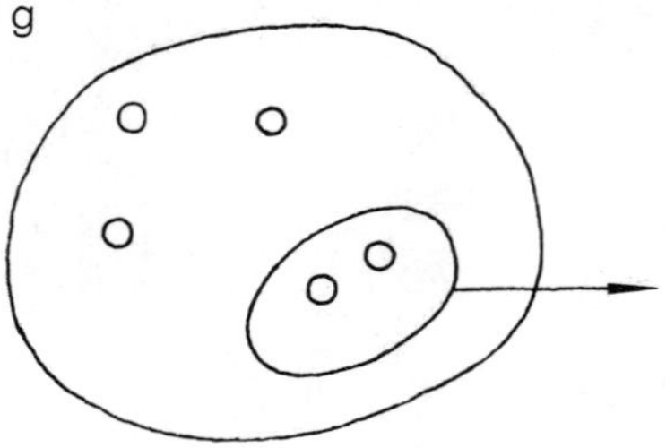

subtraction by removing a sub-set

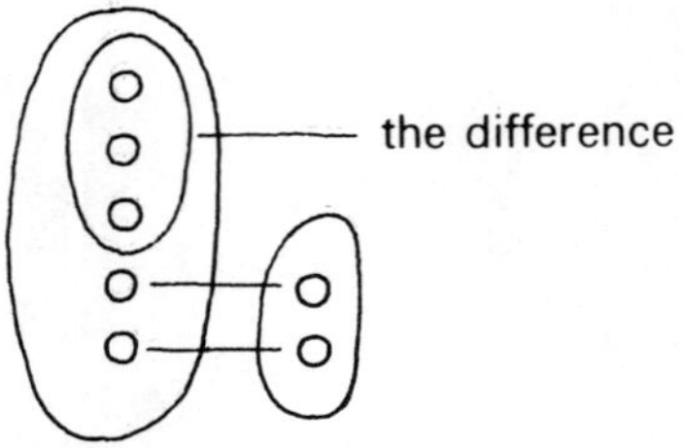

subtraction by finding the difference

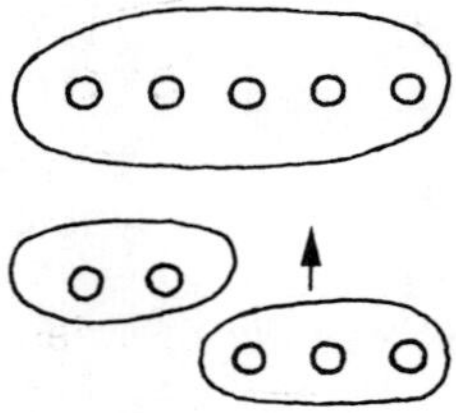

subtraction by adding on

symmetry balance about a point, line or plane.
triangle plane shape with three sides.
volume measurement of space occupied by a solid shape.

Bibliography

Biggs, E. E. and J. R. MacLean (1969) *Freedom to learn: an active learning approach to mathematics*. Addison-Wesley.

Biggs, E. E. (1971) *Mathematics for younger children.* Macmillan.

Biggs, J. B. (1967) *Mathematics and the conditions of learning.* National Foundation for Educational Research.

Boyle, D. G. (1969) *A Student's Guide to Piaget*. Pergamon Press.

Cass, J. (1971) *The Significance of Children's Play*. Batsford.

Copeland, R. W. (1974) *How Children learn Mathematics*. 2nd ed. Collier-Macmillan.

Dienes, Z. P. (1964) *Building up Mathematics*. Hutchinson Educational.

Dienes, Z. P. (1965) *Mathematics in the Primary School*. Macmillan.

Essex County Council (1971) *The Impact of Modern Mathematics in Primary Schools*. Essex County Council.

Fletcher, H. ed. (1970) *Mathematics for Schools. Teachers' Resource—Book Level 1*. Addison-Wesley.

Furth, H. G. (1970) *Piaget for Teachers*. Prentice-Hall, New Jersey.

Hartley, R. et al (1952) *Understanding Children's Play*. Routledge and Kegan Paul.

Isaacs, S. (1932) *The Nursery Years*. Routledge and Kegan Paul.

Manchester Maths Group (1971) *Notes on Guidelines in Primary Maths*. Routledge and Kegan Paul.

Marsh, L. G. (1969) *Children explore Mathematics*. 3rd ed. A. & C. Black.

May, D. E. (1963) *Children in the Nursery School*. London University Press.

Piaget, J. and Szeminska, A. (1952) *The Child's Conception of Number*. Routledge and Kegan Paul.

Roberts, V. (1971) *Playing, Learning and Living*. A. & C. Black.

van der Eyken, W. (1967) *The Pre-School Years*. Penguin.

Williams, E. M. (1970) *Mathematics: The First Three Years*. Published jointly by W. & R. Chambers and John Murray for Nuffield Foundation and C.E.D.O.

Williams, E. M. and Shuard, H. (1976) *Primary Maths Today.* Metric ed. Longman.

Index